LATIN AMERICAN HISTORICAL DICTIONARIES SERIES
Edited by A. Curtis Wilgus

Historical Dictionary
of
Ecuador

by
Albert William Bork
and
Georg Maier

Latin American Historical Dictionaries, No. 10

The Scarecrow Press, Inc.
Metuchen, N. J.   1973

Library of Congress Cataloging in Publication Data

Bork, Albert William.
    Historical dictionary of Ecuador.

    (Latin American historical dictionaries, no. 10)
    Bibliography: p.
    1. Ecuador--Dictionaries and encyclopedias.
I. Maier, Georg, joint author. II. Title.
F3704.B67   986.6'003   73-11256
ISBN 0-8108-0638-X

TABLE OF CONTENTS

EDITOR'S FOREWORD

Historians may well exclaim "Poor Ecuador, so many problems to solve and so many difficulties to overcome!" Her national life has been marked by civil struggles, unscrupulous political and military leaders, difficult economic problems, social complications, Quechua Indian cultural adjustments, religious dissentions, and, not least, boundary disputes. Certainly no other South American country has suffered more from neighbors, individually or collectively, who have encroached on territory she once possessed. By treaty or border warfare they have progressively deprived her of lands historically claimed since 1810. Even arbitration by a third power has sometimes failed to stop her shrinking patrimony.

The authors of this Dictionary fully appreciate these manifest problems, and they have endeavored to present a panoramic view of the country from pre-Columbian days. Their assignment in preparing this Dictionary has been the same as for other contributors in this Series: to arbitrarily select material which they can justify as logical, balanced and comprehensive. The points of view of the historian and the political scientist have through teamwork been combined to produce this guide for the student of Ecuador's history.

The task of cooperation has been made easier because both authors are on the staff of Southern Illinois University. Dr. Albert William Bork, as historian and language expert, has been director of the Latin American Institute since 1958, at Carbondale; Dr. Maier, currently an associate professor, has served in the Political Science Department at Edwardsville since 1965. The former was educated at Vanderbilt, the Universities of Wisconsin and Arizona, and the Universidad Nacional in Mexico. He has taught at Arizona, Washington State College, the National University of Mexico, Mexico City College, and the University of San Marcos, Lima, Peru. For four years he was employed as Director of Personnel and Industrial Relations by the General Electric Company in Mexico. His teaching, research and publications have been in the fields of history, especially Mexico, and in the Spanish and Portuguese languages. His interest in Ecuador led to his purchase for Southern Illinois University of a private collection of Ecuadorean books and pamphlets.

Dr. Georg Maier received his graduate education at the University of Florida and at Southern Illinois University. He has competence in several European and Latin American languages, and he has traveled widely in Europe and has carried on research in Ecuador, Mexico, and Guatemala. He has contributed articles and chapters to various publications, chiefly relating to Ecuador.

This combination of knowledge, backgrounds and talents has produced a book which should have wide use by scholars and librarians. It appears as volume 10 in the series of historical dictionaries of Latin America.

A. Curtis Wilgus
Emeritus Director
School of Inter-American Studies
University of Florida

PREFACE

Under the title, <u>Historical Dictionary of Ecuador,</u> one
might expect to find only names of the most important historical figures and identifications of the places most important
in the history of the country. This, however, would not provide the range and depth of information necessary to satisfy
any but the least curious user. It is the purpose of the present book to enable the user to acquaint himself with the
general political and social organization of the country, the
principal zones of archeological investigation, and similar
matters of general interest. The reader with some knowledge
of Spanish may acquaint himself with special usages of the
language in Ecuador to a rather limited extent, as well as
identify certain native foodstuffs and natural products, and
the commonest native (chiefly Quechuan) vocables.

In the preparation of this compilation, much time and
effort was expended to establish accurate dates of births,
deaths, elections and ascents to office, and of all other hap-
penings included. In some cases where several sources
were consulted, each would differ from the other; discrepan-
cies are no doubt still present, in spite of all.

Since the Independence of the northern area of South
America which constituted the old Viceroyalty of New Granada,
and the establishment of the Union of Great Colombia (Gran
Unión Colombiana) in the 1820's, followed by the separation
of Ecuador and its establishment as a nation in 1830, the
principal activity of many Ecuadoreans has been politics.
The country's functioning as a political entity has involved
many changes and "reforms" in the constitution, and the
formation of many political parties, especially in recent
years. Contemporary politics has included the fragmentation
of the basic liberal and conservative party groups and the
formation of politically oriented labor unions. Not to include
in the Dictionary these groups and organizations would mean
that the chief ingredients of contemporary history were missing. Since one of the compilers is a specialist in government and politics, he was responsible for the preparation of
entries principally involving these areas and most of the

biographical material, especially where political figures are concerned. The other compiler has attempted to fill in the missing materials in all other areas than these. The division of labor, however, was in no wise absolute.

In addition to the alphabetical listings a number of tables and lists have been included for the convenience of users. These are the pre-Conquest rulers, pre-Incaic and Incaic; archbishops and bishops of Quito; colonial heads of government; the modern provinces and their subdivisions (cantones), with their seats of government (cabeceras); and a complete list of the presidents and presidential terms of office, including an indication as to the manner in which the succession to power took place. Principle volcanoes and other landmarks are included in their corresponding places in the alphabetical listing. Biographical data on the most prominent figures in the other lists are also found in the proper place in the alphabet.

For the person unacquainted with usage in Spanish surnames, it is always the first of the compound which determines its position in the alphabetical order, for example: José Maria Velasco Ibarra is under Velasco not Ibarra; Antonio de Elizalde y La Mar is under Elizalde, not de Elizalde nor La Mar, and so on. Some persons seldom are mentioned under their complete names, as for example, Juan León Mera (Martínez), and since León could be either a given name or a family name, one might mistakenly seek him under León. There is no alternative in such cases save to look under both headings, if the first brings no result. In the handling of information concerning present-day writers and artists, no effort has been made to be exhaustive. The same is true of many more recent events. Sheer numbers make it difficult to come up with a meaningful selection without dissatisfaction for both those included and those omitted.

Included in the bibliographical list are the principal works consulted. In seeking some of the "crumbs" of information needed, especially with regard to persons, family records in Ecuador were often sought out, as were ephemeral materials of various sorts--newspapers, for example, or clippings therefrom--which are of course not included. Persons who read Spanish can pursue most of their questions in the works listed, however. In Ecuador special thanks is due to the able bibliographer, Dr. Miguel Díaz Cueva, of Cuenca, who sought out many details personally. The compilers will be pleased to have any corrections or

additions to the data presented in this Dictionary, and hope
that it will prove as useful as intended.

Albert William Bork
Georg Maier

Southern Illinois University
Carbondale, Illinois
November 1972

HISTORICAL DICTIONARY OF ECUADOR

ABARRAJARSE.   To throw oneself upon a person, to assault.

ABOMBAR.   To rot or decay.

ACCION REVOLUCIONARIA NACIONALISTA ECUATORIANA
(ARNE).   Most reactionary of Ecuador's conservative
movements, organized in 1942, its intellectual leader is
Jorge Luna Yepéz.   ARNE's structural organization,
at its base, is composed of cells (células), each having
its own chief.   Cells of a province are directed by the
provincial chief.   Provincial chiefs along with the chiefs
who hold administrative positions comprise the National
Assembly (Asamblea Nacional), which is the supreme
authority of the party.   They also elect a national
chief (jefe nacional) bound by the party statutes and
concepts.   Members of ARNE are classified as "com-
rades of first and second rank" (camaradas de primera
y segunda fila).   Only they can vote on party affairs or
hold jobs within the party.   In addition, there are so-
called sympathizers (simpatizantes), who help the party
but are not bound by oath to it.   ARNE seeks to initiate
a four-stage revolution; first, formation of a ruling
elite (élites o cuadros de mando); second, conquest of
public and mass opinion; third, conquest of the state,
and fourth, application of its principles from the seat
of power (poder).   Although one of the oldest parties
in existence today, ARNE's numerical strength has not
appreciably increased.   The membership is confined
almost exclusively to the Sierra.   In past presidential
elections the movement has supported a coalition candidate although not necessarily a conservative (i.e.,
Velasco Ibarra in 1952).   In the 1968 election, for the
first time ARNE ran its own presidential candidate,
Jorge Crespo Toral, ARNE's titular head who ran a
poor fourth in a field of five.   He has since resigned
from the party.

ACHIOTE.   Tropical tree (Bixa orellana, L.) from the
seeds of which is taken a red coloring matter used as

11

a condiment and also widely employed among primitive peoples as a cosmetic coloring.

ACOLITARSE.   To "mooch"; to partake of another's food and drink without invitation.

ADE   see   ALIANZA DEMOCRATICA ECUATORIANA

ADMINISTRADOR.   General manager of an hacienda.

ADMINISTRATIVE CAREER LAW.   The Ecuadorean Civil Service Act, promulgated in 1964, by the governing military junta in an effort to abrogate the disruptive spoils system of political appointments that traditionally takes place with each change in the presidency.   The act includes everyone in government employ from cabinet ministers to bureaucrats, postal employees, and street sweepers.   To date it has not had much real effect.

ADN   see   ALIANZA DEMOCRATICA NACIONAL

AEDA   see   ASOCIACION ECUATORIANA DE ANTROPOLOGIA

AFAROLARSE.   To worry.

AGRICULTURAL REFORM   see   INSTITUTO ECUATORIANO DE REFORMA ...

AGUACALLA.   A kind of spineless cactus.

AGUARDIENTE.   In Ecuador, as in many other Spanish-speaking areas, the word refers to a raw liquor distilled from sugar cane.

AGUILERA MALTA, DEMETRIO.   Born, May 24, 1909, Guayaquil.   Journalist, novelist.   Most important works: Los que se van, cuentos del cholo y del montuvio (co-author with Enrique Gil Gilbert and Joaquín Gallegos Lara); Don Goyo (1933); Canal-Zone (1935); La isla virgen (1942); La caballeresa del sol (1930); Siete lunas, siete pecados (1970).   Member of the "Grupo de Guayaquil" (q. v.).

AGUIRRE, JUAN BAUTISTA.   Born, April 11, 1725, Daule, now Guayas Province.   Died, June 15, 1786, Tivoli, Italy, in exile.   Jesuit priest, professor, San Gregorio University, Quito.   Early teacher of Leibnitz's and

Descartes's works. Initiated courses in experimental physics. With the expulsion of the Jesuits from the Spanish realm, he became a professor in the university colleges of Tivoli and Ferrara, serving as rector of the latter. He was an excellent poet as well and is considered the greatest Ecuadorean literary figure of colonial times. The 1917 edition of his extant works, prepared by Gonzalo Zaldumbide, is the most complete.

AGUIRRE, MANUEL AGUSTIN. Born, July 12, 1903, Loja. Education: J. D., University of Loja. Politician, educator. Secretary of the Ecuadorean Socialist Party, 1942-47; president of Permanent Legislative Committee, 1945-46; rector, Central University of Quito, 1969; one of the foremost socialist intellectuals of Ecuador.

AIRLINES (and Aviation). Early aviation enthusiasts such as José Abel Castillo, owner of the newspaper, El Telégrafo, at Guayaquil, and the Italian pilot, Elia Liut, whom he hired, began their flights in the 1920's. The first commercial service was provided by the Ecuadorean extension of the German Colombian Air Transport (SCADTA--Sociedad Colombo-Alemana de Transportes Aéreos), beginning in 1928. The name was changed to Sociedad Ecuatoriana-Alemana de Transportes Aéreos (SEADTA) at a later date and continued to operate until the beginning of World War II, when it was forced to close for lack of gasoline and was confiscated. Charter rights were given the United States subsidiary of Pan American Airlines, Panagra, which had begun service to Ecuador in 1929. Two national flag airlines were established after World War II, Aerovías Ecuatorianas (AREA) and Compañía Ecuatoriana de Aviación (CEA), with both national and international services. Smaller companies, such as Transportes Aéreos Orientales (TAO), operate chiefly across the Andes to the isolated communities in the Oriente, also served to an extent by the Ecuadorean Air Force. Present-day service by jet is provided by national, European, and United States airlines.

ALABADO. "Praised be, " salutation used by the Indians in Ecuador instead of the usual adiós or Vaya con Dios, which originally meant "God be with you" rather than "God be praised. "

ALALC see ASOCIACION LATINOAMERICANA DE LIBRE COMERCIO

ALARCON FALCONI, RUPERTO. Born, 1900, Riobamba.
Died, August 24, 1968, Quito. Education: J. D. and
social sciences, Central University of Quito, 1924.
President of Riobamba Municipal Council; deputy on
several occasions representing Chimborazo Province;
minister of Public Works and the Treasury; ambassador to Spain, Colombia, and Mexico. Ambassador
extraordinary to Venezuela; first vice-president of the
National Constituent Assembly (1946-47); presidential
candidate of the Conservative Party (1952), (unsuccessful); founder and leader of the Popular Patriotic Party
(PPP) 1966-68.

ALBENINO, NICOLAO DE. Born, ca. 1514, Florence, Italy.
Died, after 1573, probably in Potosí, now in Bolivia.
Historian of the revolt of Gonzalo Pizarro and events
in Quito (1549).

ALBORNOZ, VICTOR MANUEL. Born, March 23, 1896,
Lima, Peru. Education: Colegio Seminario, Cuenca.
Journalist, biographer-historian; founder of La Crónica
(Cuenca), 1921-30; member of the National Academy of
History; author of many biographies of important
Ecuadoreans.

ALCALDE. Political delegate in an Indian village or anejo.

ALCEDO Y HERRERA, ANTONIO LEANDRO DE. Born,
Quito, March 14, 1735. Died, La Coruña, 1812.
Studied at the Colegio Jesuita in Panama, 1743-52.
Soldier, historian, public official. Son of Dionisio de
Alcedo y Herrera, president of the Audiencia of Quito,
whom he helped prepare a study of the fortification of
Panama. Went to Spain where he joined the Royal
Guard and served during the siege of Gibraltar, 1779;
governor of Alcira, 1783, and La Coruña, 1769;
promoted to field marshal in which capacity he sur-
rendered La Coruña to Napoleon's army, 1809. Author: Diccionario geográfico e histórico de las Indias
Orientales o América, 2 vols., 1786-89. Member of
the Royal Academy of History, 1786.

ALCEDO Y HERRERA, DIONISIO DE. Born, Madrid, 1690.
Died, Madrid, 1777. Historian, public official. Ar-
rived in the New World in 1706, accompanying the
Viceroy of Peru, Marqués de Castel-Dos-Rius. Served

as governor of Canta, 1721-24, which formed part of
that viceroyalty. President of the Audiencia of Quito,
1728-36. Governor and captain general of Tierra
Firme, 1743-49. Author: Aviso histórico, político,
geográfico con las noticias más particulares de la
América Meridional, Madrid, 1740; Compendio de la
provincia, partidos, ciudades, astilleros, ríos y puer-
tos de Guayaquil, 1741.

ALDEANOS. Villagers of the Indian population centers ad-
junct to the larger mestizo villages and towns, to
whose population they have been habitually subordinated
socially.

ALEJANDRO R., NICANOR DE JESUS. Born, December 24,
1928, Santa Elena Canton, Guayas. Educated at the
Colegio Vicente Rocafuerte of Guayaquil, the State University of Guayaquil and the Central University in
Quito, Licentiate in Social Sciences. Newspaperman,
poet. Writer for El Universo, La Prensa, and El
Telégrafo. Winner of the national poetry prize named
for Ismael Pérez Pazmiño in 1967. Author of two
books of poetry and novel, Teonilo Anzules.

ALEPANTADO. Absent-minded.

ALFANDOQUE. A type of rattle made of a piece of hollow
cane and a few pebbles, and used to mark the rhythm
of certain popular music. It is of African origin.

ALFARO Y AROSEMENA, ELOY. Born, June 25, 1842,
Montecristi (Manabí Province). Died, January 28,
1912, Quito. Education: private. Soldier, politician;
civil and military chief of Esmeraldas Province, 1880;
brigadier general, 1884; lieutenant general, 1895.
Presidency: (1) non-elected, age 53, 1895, liberal
revolution; (2) elected (Constituent Convention), age 55,
1897, one term, term ended constitutionally in 1901;
(3) non-elected, age 63, 1906, when he headed the
revolution which overthrew President Lizardo García;
(4) elected by a constituent assembly, January 2, 1907,
overthrown Aug. 11, 1911 and murdered Jan. 28, 1912.

ALIANZA DEMOCRATICA ECUATORIANA (ADE). An ad-hoc
coalition composed of every political party and movement with exception of the official Radical-Liberal
Party. The ADE was formed in 1944 and led by the

dissident radical-liberal, Francisco Arízaga Luque.
His purpose was to overthrow the government of Carlos
Alberto Arroyo del Río and usher José María Velasco
Ibarra into the presidency. This objective was ac-
complished on May 31, 1944.

ALIANZA DEMOCRATICA NACIONAL (ADN). Ad-hoc coalition of independent liberals supporting the candidacy of
José Larrea in the 1952 election.   The candidate lost.

ALIANZA POPULAR (AP). Conservative coalition which
supported the presidential candidacy of Camilo Ponce
Enríquez in 1956 and 1968.   In 1968 the coalition was
supported by two major parties, the PC and the MSC,
but its candidate lost.

ALMEIDA, GILBERTO. Born, May 30, 1928, Ibarra.
School of Fine Arts, Ibarra. Contemporary painter
who has exhibited internationally.

ALVAREZ, EUDOFILO. Born, Latacunga, 1876. Died,
Quito. Studied law at Central University of Quito.
Journalist, novelist, public official, secretary to President Eloy Alfaro, 1895; director of the National Library, political chief of the Oriente, governor of Bolívar province. Author: Ocho cartas halladas, Quito,
1903; Abelardo, Quito, 1905; Cuentos y otras cosas.

AMAÑARSE. To live together in a sort of trial marriage
relationship.

AMAZON RIVER. Mightiest river of the world, the headwaters of which are in Ecuadorean territory, discovered and explored from Quito by Don Francisco de
Orellana (q.v.) in 1541-43.   These explorations and
subsequent efforts at colonization during the colonial
period were the origin of Ecuadorean claims to large
areas east of the Andes and in the regions drained by
the Ucayali and Marañón rivers, two of the principal
northward flowing tributaries which have their origin
to the south in Peru. Subsequent readjustments of the
areas subject to the jurisdiction of Quito began in the
colonial period and included the treaty of San Ildefonso
between Spain and Portugal, October 1, 1777, whereby
the former ceded 140, 000 square kilometers to what
was to become Brazil. Some maps give the name
Amazon to the main stream as far as its union with

the Pastaza, which comes down through the Andes
from Tungurahua, but others apply to the same portion of the river the name Marañón--which is the
principal, most westerly tributary originating in Peru--
and change to the Amazon designation only at the confluence with the Napo, or even with the Putumayo
further downriver. Still others differentiate the name
of the stream at the Huallaga confluence, calling it the
Marañón from there on West.

AMBATO.   Capital of the province of Tungurahua; population (1968 est.), 75, 000.   Almost destroyed by an
earthquake in 1949, and on other occasions.

AMO.   The usual meaning of a master or "boss" was
formerly extended in Ecuador and elsewhere, to include the idea of ownership or possession of the Indian
(peasant) population in a kind of serfdom.

ANCON.   Oilfields were first developed in Ecuador in the
area near this town on the Santa Elena peninsula.

ANDEAN GROUP (Grupo Andino).   The nations in the Andes
which are signatories of the Cartagena Accord (q. v.),
but are also members of the Latin American Free
Trade Association (see Asociación Latinoamericana...).
They are: Ecuador, Colombia, Peru, Chile, and
Bolivia.   Venezuela was originally included but has
only recently become a signatory.

ANDRADE, CARLOS VICENTE.   Born, September 15, 1915,
Cotocachi.   School of Fine Arts, Quito.   Painter.

ANDRADE, ROBERTO.   Born, 1852, Havana, Cuba.   Died,
1938.   Historian.   Wrote especially on Juan de Montalvo and García Moreno.

ANDRADE COELLO, ALEJANDRO.   Born, December 28,
1888, Quito.   Educated in Quito and the Pedagogical
Institute in Santiago de Chile.   Journalist and professor.   Editor of El Comercio.   Professor of literature
and hygiene in the National Institute "Mejía del Valle"
in Quito.   Member of many academies and learned
societies.   Author: various biographical and critical
literary studies.   Founder of the Revista Nacional,
El Educador, Albores Literarios.

ANDRADE CORDERO, CESAR. Born, 1905, Cuenca. Poet.

ANDRADE FAINI, CESAR. Born, 1913, Quito. School of
Fine Arts, Quito. Contemporary painter and professor
of painting in Guayaquil.

ANDRADE MARIN, FRANCISCO. Born, February 15, 1841,
Ibarra. Died, September 26, 1935, Quito. Education:
J. D., Central University, Quito. Lawyer, politician.
Member of the Municipal Council of Quito; member of
the Council of State; deputy from Manabí Province to
the 1883 Constituent Convention; minister of Public
Works, 1892; minister of the Treasury; president of
the Chamber of Deputies, 1911. Presidency: non-
elected, age 71, 1912, succeeding Carlos Freile
Zaldumbide, when the latter, who as president of the
Chamber of Deputies had taken over at the time of
the assassination of Eloy Alfaro, resigned. When
Freile left the Chamber of Deputies, Andrade Marín
succeeded to the presidency of that body, and thus was
next in line for the position of president of the nation
under the constitution then in force. Once is office
he called for elections and was succeeded by Leónidas
Plaza Gutiérrez.

ANDRADE MARIN, LUCIANO. Born, January 27, 1893,
Quito. Education: doctorate (honoris causa), Central
University of Quito, 1937. Historian, educator.
Director of Municipal Library in Quito, 1917-19;
director of Agricultural School in Ambato, 1919-22;
owner of the Equinoxial Museum in Quito, 1956.

ANDRADE MOSCOSO, JAIME. Born in 1913, Quito. Contemporary Ecuadorean sculptor.

ANDULLO. Leaf tobacco, wrapped in its own leaves for
export.

ANEJO. Literally, "annex," but used in Ecuador in the
sense of a village where the inhabitants are almost
exclusively Indians, as opposed to the inhabitants of
the cabecera, head of a political or church district,
who are largely white or mestizo, consider themselves
superior, and are known as gente del pueblo (towns-
people).

ANGOSTURA, CONGRESS OF. In December 1819 a Con-

stituent Congress met in Angostura (Venezuela) and
elected Simón Bolívar as the president of Gran Colombia, composed of Venezuela, New Granada, and the
Presidence of Quito (Ecuador). Bolívar was to assume
his position after these territories had been liberated.

AÑO VIEJO.   Puppet made of rags symbolizing the old year.
Burned on the night of December 31, the puppet is
made by people who dress in black and put on a mask.
They represent the widows of the "Old Year" and carry
their puppet to the street and burn it at the appropriate
time.   On so doing they ask passersby for a donation
"for the poor old man who is about to die."

ANSIATICO.   Hungry, anxious.

ANSP   see   ASOCIACION NACIONAL DE SERVIDORES
PUBLICOS

ANTE, ANTONIO.   Born, January 1771, Quito.   Died, 1836,
Quito.   Education: J.D., University of Quito.   Lawyer.   Precursor of Ecuador's independence; deputy to
the 1830 Constituent Convention in Riobamba when
Ecuador was declared a Republic.   Exiled to Africa in
1816 after a Royalist attempt to assassinate him had
failed, he was able to return to Ecuador and public
life after independence was won.

ANTEPARA, JOSE DE.   Born, 1770, Guayaquil.   Died,
September 12, 1821, Huachi.   Insurrectionist, 1820,
at Guayaquil.   Became a captain in the fight against
the Royalists.   Killed in battle.

ANTIZANA.   Volcano located in the eastern Cordillera and
visible from Quito.   Elevation, 18,714 feet.

AP   see   ALIANZA POPULAR

APACHITA.   Name given to a type of roadside shrine which
developed at resting places along the roads in colonial
times.   Indians would leave offerings of various types,
such as coca leaves, feathers of birds, and other
articles.

APEGADO.   "Attached" relatives of small Indian families
who own land but live in separate households.

APU.   Individual who acts as intermediary between the
   Indians, the parish priest, and the political lieutenant.
   The office of apu exists today primarily in the highland region around the City of Riobamba.   Hereditary
   and dating back to the Inca period, the position represents the only element in the social structure which,
   in theory at least, would allow the Indian some means
   of representation in a system where he had no recognition as a human being and no rights.

ARAUJO HIDALGO, MANUEL.   Born, 1921, Carchi.   Education: J. D. University of Buenos Aires.   Politician.
   Member of ARNE until 1955; minister of Government,
   1960; organizer of the Revolutionary Front of Popular
   Organizations (FROP), 1968; deputy from Pichincha
   Province, 1968.   A self-styled revolutionary who sometimes admires Fidel Castro.

ARAUJO Y RIO, JOSE DE.   Born, Lima.   Public official.
   President of the Audiencia of Quito, to which he was
   appointed May 16, 1732, but did not take possession
   until December 8, 1736.   He was deposed in 1743.
   His chief clerk (requisidor), don Manuel Rubio de
   Arévalo, acted temporarily as his substitute.   Araujo
   returned to the presidency, which he occupied until
   becoming president of the Audiencia of Guatemala.

ARCHIDONA.   Village founded by Gil Ramírez Dávalos on
   the eastern slopes of the Andes in 1560.

ARCHIPIELAGO DE COLON   see   GALAPAGOS ISLANDS

ARENAS, JUAN PABLO   see   MONTUFAR Y LARREA ...

ARIZAGA LUQUE, FRANCISCO.   Born, January 6, 1900,
   Piura, Peru.   Died, 1964, Quito.   Education: J. D.
   University of Guayaquil.   Lawyer, politician.   Minister
   of Public Education; member of Governing Junta, 1925;
   leader of Ecuadorean Democratic Alliance (ADE) which
   overthrew President Arroyo del Río and ushered
   Velasco Ibarra into office, 1946.   Vice-President,
   1946.

ARMENDARIZ, LOPE AUX DIEZ DE   see   AUX DIEZ DE
   ARMENDARIZ, LOPE

ARMENDARIZ, LOPE DIAZ DE   see   DIAZ DE ARMENDA-
   RIZ, LOPE

ARMENDARIZ, LUIS. Born, Quito. Brother of Lope Díaz de Armendáriz. Doctor of theology, University of St. Thomas Acquinas, Quito. Clergyman, public official. He joined the order of St. Bernard, and later became bishop of Jaén de Bracamoros, archbishop of Tarragona, and finally, viceroy of Cataluña, thus probably attaining higher office than any other Spaniard born in the New World.

ARNE see ACCION REVOLUCIONARIA ...

AROSEMENA GOMEZ, OTTO. Born, July 19, 1925, Guayaquil. Education: University of Guayaquil, law. Professor, lawyer, politician. President of the Provincial Electoral Tribunal (Guayas Province); deputy from Guayas Province to the National Congress. President of Chamber of Deputies; functional senator for commerce representing the Coast; twice vice-president of the Senate; interim president of the Republic (1966-68); founder of the Democratic Institutionalist Coalition (CID), a center-right oriented party in 1965.

AROSEMENA MONROY, CARLOS JULIO. Born, August 24, 1919. Education: J. D. University of Guayaquil, 1945. Lawyer, politician; counsellor of Ecuadorean Embassy in Washington, D. C., 1945-46; deputy from Guayas Province, 1952 and 1958; president of the Chamber of Deputies; vice-president of the Republic 1960-61; deputy from Guayas Province to the Constituent Convention of 1967; deputy from Guayas Province, 1968. Presidency: non-elected, age 42, 1961, succeeding José María Velasco Ibarra, after he was overthrown. Arosemena Monroy was himself overthrown in 1963 by a military junta.

AROSEMENA TOLA, CARLOS JULIO. Born, 1894, Guayaquil. Died, February 20, 1952, Guayaquil. Education: Cornell University (USA). Banker, politician. Presidency: elected, age 53 (Special Congressional Convention), 1947, interim president who took over after the resignation of Mariano Suárez Veintimilla and served until elections could be called in 1948.

ARRANQUITIS. Poverty.

ARRIOLA BELARDI, MARTIN DE. Born, San Sebastián. Died, Quito, 1593. Licenciate in law. University of

Salamanca, 1625. Knight of the order of Alcántara.
Public official, lawyer. Magistrate of Charcas, 1628
and Lima, 1634; president of the Audiencia of Quito,
1646-53.

ARRIVISMO. Use of influence or underhanded practices to
obtain public employment.

ARROYO DEL RIO, CARLOS ALBERTO. Born, November
27, 1893, Guayaquil. Died, October 31, 1969, Guayaquil. Education: J. D. University of Guayaquil, 1914.
Lawyer, politician; secretary of the Guayaquil Municipal Council, 1917-18; deputy from Guayas Province,
1922-23; president of the Chamber, 1923; president of
the Senate, 1939. Presidency: (1) non-elected, age
45, 1939; took over after the death of President
Aurelio Mosquera Narváez, left office to campaign in
the forthcoming elections; (2) elected (popular), age
47, 1940, one term, was overthrown in 1944.

ARTETA Y CALISTO, NICOLAS JOAQUIN DE. Born, Quito,
1771. Died, Quito, September 1849. J. D. University
of Quito. Lawyer, clergyman. Rector of the University of Quito; vice-president of the Constituent Assembly of 1830; dean of the Faculty of Law. Bishop of
Quito, 1835-49; first archbishop of Quito, 1849-51.

ARTETA Y CALISTO, PEDRO JOSE DE. Born, March,
1797, Quito. Died, August 24, 1873, Quito. Education: J. D. University of Santo Tomás, Quito; lawyer,
politician. Deputy in 1822 Congress of Gran Colombia;
deputy in constituent Assembly at Riobamba, 1830; co-
signer of the 1832 boundary agreement with Colombia;
vice-president of the Republic, 1867-69. Interim
president, age 63, November 1867 to January 1868.

ASCASUBI, FRANCISCO JAVIER DE. Born, Quito. Died,
August 2, 1810, Quito. Early leader in anti-Spanish
movement. Leader in a disastrous battle at Sapuyes,
October 16, 1809, he was captured and shot "while
trying to escape jail" in Quito.

ASCASUBI, MANUEL. Born, December 1804, Quito. Died,
December 25, 1876, Quito. Military career, rank of
colonel, politician; substitute senator from Chimborazo
Province, 1846; governor of Imbabura and Pichincha
Provinces; vice-president of the Republic, 1847;

minister of War; minister of Interior. Presidency:
(1) non-elected, age 45, 1849, when he took office
because Congress could not decide on a successor to
Vicente Ramón Roca, and served until 1850; (2) non-
elected, age 71, 1875, replaced Francisco Javier
León had taken over after assassination of Gabriel
García Moreno.

ASENTANTE. A liquor which is drunk to celebrate a
fortunate business deal or a piece of good news.
From asentar, to settle, as of the turbulence in a
cloudy liquid, or of the foundation of a house.

ASOCIACION ECUATORIANA DE ANTROPOLOGIA (AEDA).
Founded by Dr. Antonio Santiana and Dr. Silvio Luis
Haro, later bishop of Ibarra, on November 22, 1947,
on the occasion of the celebration at Riobamba of the
bi-centenary of the birth of Pedro Vicente Maldonado.
It has sections devoted to Ethnology, Folklore, Linguis-
tics, Archeology, Social Anthropology, and Physical
Anthropology. The official address of the association
is now in Quito, in the Ethnographic Museum of the
Central University, where it has a government subsidy.

ASOCIACION LATINOAMERICANA DE LIBRE COMERCIO
(ALALC). Free trade commission developed at
Punta del Este, Uruguay, meeting in 1967, that works
for regional agreements.

ASOCIACION NACIONAL DE SERVIDORES PUBLICOS (ANSP).
Founded in 1964 after the governing military junta had
decreed the "Administrative Career Law" of the same
year. All employees in the various ministries are
members of the Association. Exercises little if any
power as a pressure group since chief executives are
still employing the spoils system to reward their
friends.

ASOROCHARSE. To become ill with the "soroche" or
"altitude sickness."

ASQUEAR. Of animals or domestic fowls, to abandon their
young; of persons, to break away from friends, cease
to show confidence in another.

ATACAMES. Archeological area located primarily on the
coast of Esmeraldas Province, dated between A.D. 500
and 1500.

ATAHUALPA (Atahuallpa, Atabalipa). Born 1502, died 1533.
The last Inca (chieftain), king of Quito. Half brother
of Huáscar, Inca of Peru, with whom he waged civil
war when Francisco Pizarro, the Spanish conqueror
reached the region. Huáscar was defeated by Atahualpa, but the Inca empire was so weakened that the
Spaniards were able to conquer it. Atahualpa was
made a prisoner and his principal military leaders
were killed by the Spaniards when he refused to ac-
knowledge Charles I of Spain as his sovereign and
become a Christian. He kept the promise of a room-
ful of gold ($8,000,000) as a ransom, but was con-
demned to death for alleged crimes and strangled on
August 29, 1533.

AUCA. Indian tribe occupying the Oriente region between
the rivers Napo and Curaray. Known for their ferocity,
the Aucas number around 600, most of whom are presently integrated due to the efforts of the Instituto
Lingüístico de Verano. Only a group of 250 remain
untouched by civilization.

AUDIENCIA see REAL AUDIENCIA

AUX DIEZ DE ARMENDARIZ, LOPE. Born, Navarre,
Spain. Public official. President of the Audiencia
of Quito, 1571-1574. He later served as president
of the Audiencia of Charcas (Bolivia). Father of
Lope Díaz de Armendáriz and Luis de Armendáriz,
both of whom were born at Quito and achieved positions of importance in the government of the Spanish
empire.

AVIATION see AIRLINES

AYAHUASCA. Banisteria caapi, also called bejuco del
muerto, a liana from the leaves of which the Indians
of Eastern Ecuador make a hallucinogenic tea. It is
widely used by witch doctors and herbalists.

AYAMPACO. A kind of tamal made of green banana with
fish and condiments. It is wrapped in banana leaves
before baking in the oven.

AYMERICH, MELCHOR. Last president of the Audiencia of
Quito, April-May 1822. Defeated at the battle of
Pichincha on May 24, 1822, by the republic forces of
Antonio José de Sucre.

AYORA, ISIDRO. Born, August 31, 1879, Loja. Education:
M. D., Central University of Quito, 1905. Physician,
educator, politician. Professor at Central University
of Quito, 1912; rector of the same university, 1925;
minister of Social Security, 1926; member of the Provisional Junta, January 10, 1926 to March 31, 1926.
Presidency: (1) non-elected, age 47, 1926; he convoked a Constituent Convention, 1929; (2) elected to
succeed himself, but resigned in favor of General
Luis Larrea Alba in 1931, before completing his term
in office.

AYUDA. As a masculine noun, Indian hireling, worker.

AZOGUES. Capital of the Province of Cañar. Population
(1968 est.) 10,000. Major center for mining of coal,
mercury, copper, gold, silver, sulphur, and platinum.
The name is a Spanish word for mercury.

AZUAY. Province, Southwestern Ecuador. Area, 3,211
square miles. The population is largely Indian living
from agriculture, weaving, lace making, pottery, and
the manufacture of Panama hats. Population (1968
est.) 306,700. Cuenca, the capital, is often referred
to as the "city of poets."

- B -

BABAHOYO. Capital of the Province of Los Ríos. Population (1968 est.), 25,000.

BABAHOYO RIVER. A stream which originates southeast
of Quevedo and flows through most of Los Ríos Province
to enter the sea in the Gulf of Guayaquil.

BACALAO. "Ugly woman" (literally, codfish).

BADULAQUE. Dishonest person, or one who is not depend-
able.

BAEZA. Settlement founded by Gil Ramírez Dávalos on the
eastern slopes of the Andes in 1559.

BAHIA. Archeological zone situated on the Ecuadorean coast
from the latitude of La Plata Island northward to the
Bahía de Caráquez. It dates back to the first century

B. C. , and is very rich in pottery and ceramic figures.
The Bahía phase differs from other phases of the similar period in the presence of several types of carved
stone objects.

BANANA. This tropical fruit has been Ecuador's largest
source of foreign exchange since 1951. Since 1953,
Ecuador has been the largest exporter of bananas in
the world, a position it will most likely cede to Hon-
duras in the near future. The variety commonly grown
is called Gros-Michel. Other varieties such as the
Cavendish, Lacatan, and Valery have a four to five
times larger yield than the former and are also immune to the Panamá disease. However, they have not
been grown in sufficient quantity in Ecuador.

BANDA MOCHA. A musical group, chiefly percussions, but
aside from a flute of indigenous design, and a type of
drum (bombo), it has no true musical instruments.
The blade of a machete, various kinds of hardened
leaves from tropical trees, or empty steel containers,
are among the items used. It is common among the
population of African origin.

BAQUERIZO MORENO, ALFREDO. Born, September 28,
1859, Guayaquil. Died, March 20, 1951, New York.
Education: J. D. , 1884. Lawyer, politician, novelist.
Director of the Public Library and mayor of Guayaquil,
1890-96; secretary to the minister of the Superior
Court in Guayaquil, 1894-1901; minister of Foreign
Relations, 1902-12; minister in Cuba, and ambassador
to Peru, 1903-1907; vice-president and president of
the Republic, 1903-1906; senator from Guayas Province
and president of the Senate, 1912-16. Presidency:
(1) elected (popular), age 57, 1916, one term which
ended constitutionally in 1920; (2) non-elected, age 72,
1931, took over from General Luis Larrea Alba, whose
desire to rule as a dictator was not acceptable to the
people, and served until 1932. His psychological novels,
El señor Penco, and Tierra adentro are best known.
He also wrote verse and essays.

BARROS DE SAN MILLAN, MANUEL. Born, Segovia,
Spain. Died, Quito, 1599. Public official. President
of the Audiencia of Quito, 1587-93. He entered the city
to take possession of the office, August 2, 1587.
During his term (1592) an uprising in protest against

the imposition of the <u>alcabala</u> (a kind of sales tax) took place.

BATTLE OF PICHINCHA   see   PICHINCHA, BATTLE OF

BELLO, ANDRES. Born, November 30, 1780, Caracas, Venezuela. Died, October 15, 1865, Santiago de Chile. Poet, jurisconsult, philologist, philosopher, politician. Although never long in Ecuador, Bello is regarded as a national cultural and political hero because of his association with Bolívar in the movement for independence and because of his friendship with José Joaquín Olmedo (q. v.). His <u>Principles of International Law</u> was long the standard university text, and his grammar of the Spanish language, later revised and completed by Rufino José Cuervo, is still one of the standard reference works on the subject. His poetry is still read and recited in most Spanish American schools. He served as arbiter in a dispute between the U. S. and Ecuador.

BENALCAZAR, SEBASTIAN DE [also, Belalcázar]. Born, 1495, Benalcázar, Spain. Died, 1550, Cartagena, Colombia. Real name, Sebastián Moyano. Spanish soldier of fortune who conquered Quito in December 1533, after having defeated Atahualpa's general Rumiñahui. Benalcázar traveled east in search of El Dorado in 1536, and became governor of Popayán, now in Colombia, in 1538.

BENITEZ VINUEZA, LEOPOLDO. Born, October 17, 1905, Guayaquil. Education: licentiate in political science, University of Guayaquil. Diplomat, novelist-historian. Deputy to 1944-45 Constitutional Convention. Ambassador to Uruguay, Bolivia, Argentina and the United States. Author: <u>El zapador de la Colonia,</u> 1941; <u>La vida y la obra de Francisco Xavier Espejo</u>, 1941; <u>Argonautas de la selva</u> (biography of Captain D. Francisco de Orellana and the discovery of the Amazon), 1945; <u>Ecuador: drama y paradoja</u>, 1950.

BIJA. Equivalent of <u>achiote</u> in some areas.

"BLACK CHARTER" see CONSTITUTIONS

BOLIVAR. Province in the west-central part of Ecuador. Area, 1288 square miles. Major products of the province are chinchona bark, timber and agricultural products. Capital, Guaranda. Population: (1968 est.) 166, 600.

BOLIVAR, SIMON. Born, July 12, 1783, Caracas, Venezuela. Died, December 17, 1830, Santa Marta, Colombia. Soldier-statesman to whom Ecuador owes its independence. In the Ecuadorean campaign Bolívar was assisted by the most brilliant of his officers, Antonio José de Sucre, who defeated the Spaniards at the battle of Pichincha on May 24, 1822. The victory freed Ecuador from Spanish domination. In July 1822 Bolívar met San Martín and took over leadership of all patriot forces. It was in Quito that Bolívar met the first passion of his life, Manuela Sáenz, who followed him from camp to battle field and even to the presidential palace.

BOLSICON. Full skirt reaching halfway to the ankles, usually of coarse cotton or wool, and with an embroidered border. From this skirt the women were called bolsiconas. Worn by the women of the popular masses, the bolsicón formed one of the three garments which clothed them. The others were a shirtwaist, and a kind of shawl. Since they were barefoot, the name llapangas was also applied to the women of the populace, from ñapa (Quechua) bare or naked. Also, ñapanga.

BONIFAZ ASCASUBI, NEPTALI. Born, December 29, 1870. Died, Quito, 1960?. Educated at the Jesuit College of Quito, in Geneva, Switzerland, and at the Sorbónne in Paris, he resided abroad for many years, especially from 1908 to 1925. Upon his return to Quito he became president of the Central Bank of Ecuador. When his candidacy was proposed in the 1931 presidential elections it was backed by a coalition of conservatives, liberals and socialists, the Unión Patriótica Nacional. Bonifaz was victorious, having obtained 28, 359 of the 60, 820 votes cast in a hotly contested election in which three candidates sought the office. Modesto Larrea Jijón, the next highest, received 18, 863. Bonifaz did not occupy the presidency, however, because the National Congress after a long and bitter contest pro and con in the newspapers of the country, and several uprisings in which lives were lost and blood was shed, voted 46-38 on August 19, 1932, to disqualify him.

He was certified president-elect, but disqualified because of his birth in the Peruvian Embassy. He was
a son of a Peruvian diplomat, and an Ecuadorean
mother, and until 1916 when he was 46 years of age
he always declared his citizenship to be Peruvian.
There ensued a period of great tension both among the
supporters and opponents of Bonifaz, and finally an
armed confrontation and hostilities known as the "Four
Days' War" in and around Quito, in the course of which
more than 200 members of the armed forces and
civilians were killed and many more wounded.

BORGES Y NAJERA, ALBERTO.   Born, San Sebastián,
Spain.   Educated in Spain, France, and Belgium.
Retired ship's captain.   Publisher of the magazine,
Vistazo, Television newscaster.   Movie director.
War correspondent.   Winner of several awards inter-
nationally in all of the mass media.   Author of three
novels.

BORJA, ARTURO.   Born, Quito, 1892.   Died, November 13,
1912, Quito.   Poet of the Modernist group.   Born of a
socially prominent family, he started writing verse
while quite young.   When he died at the age of 20, it
was collected and published posthumously, in a small
volume titled, La Flauta de Onix.

BORJA, CESAR.   Born, 1852, Guayaquil.   Died, 1910.
Education: M.S., University of San Marcos, Lima.
Public official, physician, poet.   Served in various
government offices, including minister of Public Instruction.   Besides writing as a participant in the
"modernist" movement in Ecuadorean poetry, he
translated Leconte de Lisle, Heredia, Baudelaire and
Verlaine.

BORJA PEREZ, LUIS FELIPE.   Born, February 20, 1845,
Quito.   Died, April 13, 1912, Quito.   Education:
J.D., University of Quito, 1869.   Lawyer, politician.
Elected to Municipal Council of Quito, 1875; professor of law, University of Quito, 1878; deputy from the
Province of León to the nation's Congress, 1883; rector of University of Quito, 1895; senator from Esmeraldas Province, 1904; president of the Law Academy,
1910.   One of the most important Liberals of 19th-
century Ecuador, he conspired against President García
Moreno and was named to the directorate of the Radical-

Liberal Party when it held its first national assembly
in 1890.

BORJA Y BORJA, RAMIRO. Born, June 23, 1920, Quito.
Education: J. D. , Central University of Quito, 1949.
Lawyer, professor of constitutional law. President of
the Legislative Commission, 1958-63. Author: Las
constituciones del Ecuador, 1951; Derecho constitucional ecuatoriano, 1950; Constitución quiteña, 1962.

BORRERO, MANUEL MARIA. Born, 1883, Cuenca. Education: J. D. Author, lawyer, politician, minister of
the Superior Court in Quito; deputy from Azuay Province; Ecuadorean consul in Valparaíso (Chile); governor
of Azuay Province; minister of the Supreme Court.
Presidency: non-elected, age 52, 1938, interim president for less than three months.

BORRERO Y CORTAZAR, ANTONIO. Born, October 28,
1827, Cuenca. Died, October 9, 1911, Cuenca. Education: J. D. , University of Cuenca, 1856. Lawyer,
politician. Vice-president of the Republic, 1863;
secretary of the Bishopric, Cuenca, 1872; minister of
the Superior Court in Azuay Province, 1874; governor
of Azuay Province, 1888-92. Presidency: elected
(popular), age 48, 1875, one term, overthrown by
General Ignacio de Veintimilla in 1876.

BOUGUER, PIERRE. Born, February 16, 1688, Croisic,
Brittany. Died, August 15, 1758, Paris. French
member of the Condamine expedition (q. v.). Mathe-
matician, inventor of photometry and the heliometer.

BRAVO, PIO. Born, 1804, Cuenca. Died, February 20,
1858, Cuenca. Education: J. D. , University of St.
Thomas, Quito. Lawyer, politician. Served in Congress representing his province. Member of the 1845
Constituent Convention. "Champion of the trial by
jury" system in criminal cases.

BUCARAM ELMHALIN, ASAAD. Born, June, 1921, Ambato.
Politician. Mayor of Guayaquil, 1962; deputy from
Guayas 1966; head of the Concentration of Popular
Forces (CFP), 1965. Joined FID coalition support
of Andrés F. Córdova Nieto in 1968 presidential election. Prefect of Guayas Province, 1970. Leading
candidate for president, 1972, eliminated when a junta

under General Guillermo Rodríguez Lara took over the government.

- C -

CAAMAÑO Y CORNEJO, JOSE MARIA PLACIDO. Born, October 5, 1838, Guayaquil. Died, December 31, 1901, Sevilla, Spain. Education: J. D. , Central University of Quito. Lawyer, politician, general commander of the 2nd Division, 1883; member of the Provisional Government, July 9, 1883 to February 9, 1884; minister plenipotentiary to the United States, 1888; governor of Guayas Province, 1888-1895. Presidency: elected (Constituent Convention), age 46, 1884, one term which ended constitutionally in 1888.

CABECERA. "Head town" where the parish priest (cura), teniente politico, apú, the church, jail, and the local administrative and judicial offices, all are located. The word applies to the administrative center both of a parroquia and of a cantón.

CABILDO. Town council; governing council in an Indian settlement (comuna).

CABUYA. In Ecuadorean usage the Agave americana or a related species, from the fibrous leaves of which twine is made; and from the juice, various beverages. The fibre is also used to weave coarse cloth bags.

CACAHUERO. Urban cacao workers who are employed by the cacao exporter for the purpose of re-sunning, bagging, and loading the cacao.

CACAO. The cacao bean is native to the eastern slopes of the Ecuadorean Andes and Ecuador was known as the producer of the world's finest cacao and the world's leading exporter between 1894 and 1905. Four major varieties were grown which in order of decreasing quality were known as Nacional Arriba, Balao, Machala, and Bahía de Caráquez--according to the respective zones of production.

CACAO NACIONAL ARRIBA. The finest grade of cacao grown in Ecuador and perhaps in the whole world. It is grown in the province of Los Ríos along the

Babahoyo and Daule rivers.

CACHULLAPI.   A popular dance form in the Andes.

CADENA, LUIS.   Born, January 12, 1830, Quito.   Died,
    March 24, 1906.   Painter.   After a number of years
    in Chile, he studied in Europe at government expense
    and then returned to establish an Academy of Fine
    Arts, which, however, did not prosper, because upon
    the death of García Moreno, it was closed.   He had
    several sons who succeeded him in activities in the
    various plastic arts.   Congress voted him a life pen-
    sion in 1902.

CAICEDO, MANUEL JOSE.   Historian of the Independence
    movement, 1809-1810.

CALDERON, FRANCISCO [also, Francisco García Calderón].
    Born, 1765, Havana, Cuba.   Dicd, December 3, 1812,
    Ibarra (firing squad).   Precursor of Ecuador's Inde-
    pendence.   Father of Abdón Calderón (next entry).

CALDERON GARAICOA, ABDON ZENON.   Born, July 30,
    1804, Cuenca.   Died, May 25, 1822, Quito.   Of noble
    family, son of Francisco García Calderón and Manuela
    Garaicoa y Olmedo, he joined the military in the in-
    dependence movement, 1820.   He fought in the first
    battle at Huachi, and distinguished himself in the bat-
    tle of Pichincha, May 24, 1822.   Badly wounded, he
    died the next day.   He has gone down in Ecuadorean
    history as a patriot and hero.   He was posthumously
    awarded the rank of captain.

CALICUCHIMA.   One of the Inca Atahualpa's most important
    generals who with Quisquis defeated Huascar's army
    and conquered Peru.   When Atahualpa was imprisoned
    by the Spaniards he delivered to them 35 pieces
    (100 lbs.) of gold.   Condemned by the Spaniards as
    a traitor, he died at the stake in 1553.

CALLAHUAZO, JACINTO.   Born, near Ibarra, 18th century.
    An Indian cacique of noble heritage who dedicated his
    life to the study of the history of his country.   At age
    30 he wrote a book: Las guerras civiles del Inca
    Atahualpa con su hermano Atoco, llamado Huascar
    Inca.   Unfortunately the work was destroyed by the
    Spanish and Callahuazo was thrown in jail.   At age 80,

he wrote a resume of the same work which was read
by Father Juan de Velasco and highly praised in his
Historia del reino de Quito.

LA CALLE. Monthly political magazine published in Quito
with a circulation of 2000. It was founded on March
14, 1957 and has a center-left editorial policy. Its
director is Carlos Enrique Carrión.

CALLE, MANUEL DE JESUS. Born, December, 1866,
Cuenca. Died, October 6, 1918, Guayaquil. Literary
critic, journalist, historian, politician. One of the
most important journalists in Ecuador's history.
Founder of many journals and newspapers. He used
the pseudonyms Ernesto Mora and Enrique de Restignac.

CALVETE DE ESTRELLA, JUAN CRISTOBAL. Born, ca.
1525, Saviñena (Huesca), Spain. Died, 1593, Salamanca. Humanist, historian. Wrote of the period of
Gonzalo Pizarro in Ecuador. The Latin manuscript
of his work has for many years awaited publication as
a whole.

CAMARA DE AGRICULTURA. The Chamber of Agriculture,
established February 10, 1938, by President Alberto
Enríquez Gallo. Its purpose is to help in agricultural
development and cooperate with the government in the
study and resolution of agricultural and economic problems. Structurally the Chamber is organized into
three zones: the first zone includes the seven Andean
provinces of Bolívar, Carchi, Chimborazo, Cotopaxi,
Imbabura, Pichincha, and Tungurahua; the second
embraces the five coastal provinces of El Oro, Esmeraldas, Guayas, Los Ríos, and Manabí; and the
third, the three Andean provinces of Azuay, Cañar,
and Loja, as well as the four provinces of the Oriente:
Morona-Santiago, Napo, Pastaza, and Zamora-Chinchipe. Each zone elects its own president. Agriculture is also represented in Congress by two functional
senators, one representing the agricultural interest of
the Costa (i. e., zone 2) and one representing the
Sierra and the Oriente (i. e., zones 1 and 3).

CAMARA DE COMERCIO. The Chamber of Commerce was
established on January 5, 1938, by President Alberto
Enríquez Gallo. The purpose is to foment development
and to solve commercial problems in cooperation with

the government.   The meaning of "commerce" here is
the very broad one of all trades and cannot be considered an exact parallel to the U. S. Chamber of Commerce.   Structurally the Chamber has offices in each
provincial capital as well as in each county (cantón)
where the economic situation requires it.   Commercial
interests are represented in Congress by two functional
senators, selected one each from the Costa and Sierra.

CAMARA DE INDUSTRIA.   The Chamber of Industry was
established on August 20, 1936, by President Federico
Páez.   Its purpose is to foment development and to
solve industrial problems in cooperation with the government.   Structurally, the Chamber has offices in
every provincial capital as well as in each county
(cantón), where the economic situation requires it.
Industrial interests enjoy functional representation in
the Senate.   One senator each from the Costa and
Sierra is elected to represent these interests.

CAMARI.   Gift of grain, chickens, and other produce be-
stowed by the highland Indian on the hacendado, and
even sometimes on the mayorales and mayordomo, in
an annual exchange.   The recipient usually gives chicha,
brandy and food.

CAMPO, ANTONIO DEL.   Born, Guayaquil, 20th-century
painter, recognized for the originality of his techniques
and his depth of feeling.

CAÑAR.   Province in the south-central Ecuadorean highlands.
Area 1614 square miles.   Population (1968 est.),
129, 000.   Capital, Azogues.

CAÑARI.   Archeological region located in the southern highlands, primarily in the Cuenca, Cañar, and Alausí
basins.   Named after the Cañari tribe, the phase dates
from after A. D. 500 to 1500.   There is an abundance
of gold and copper objects, stone tools, and well-made
pottery.

CAÑARI.   The principal Indian nation in southern Ecuador,
occupying a large area in the Sierra and the western
lowlands at the time of the Spanish conquest.

CAÑIZARES, MANUELA.   Famous patriot of Quito in whose
house the first proclamation of independence was made

on August 10, 1809. A patriotic junta was formed with
the following officers: President Juan Pío Montúfar y
Larrea, Marqués de Selva Alegre; Vice-President
Bishop José Cuero y Caicedo; Secretary of Internal
Affairs Dr. Juan de Dios Morales; Secretary of Justice
Dr. Manuel Rodríguez de Quiroga; and Secretary of
the Treasury Juan Larrea. The junta was dissolved on
October 28, 1809. Manuela Cañizares was tried for
treason and condemned to execution by a firing squad
in 1810, but it is not known whether the sentence was
ever carried out. Her will, dated August 27, 1814,
has been found, however.

CANTON. Political subdivision, which with relation to the
provinces in Ecuador, corresponds to a county in the
United States. A canton usually takes its name from
the principal town which would be like a county seat.
See Appendix 8, a list of provinces and their cantons.

CAPAC URCU. Quechua name for the volcano, Altar, meaning "Bright Mountain. "

CAPE SAN FRANCISCO. In Esmeraldas Province at the
mouth of the short San Francisco River, it forms the
land barrier which creates the Ensenada of the same
name, a not very extensive and open cove on the Pacific
Ocean.

CARA. Archeological region located in the northern highlands, primarily in the Quito and Ibarra basins.
Named after the Cara tribe, the phase dates from
after A. D. 500 to 1500.

CARA. Indian tribe inhabiting Imbabura and northe.n
Pichincha Province at the time of the Spanish conquest.
According to the historian, Juan de Velasco, the Caras
came from some place beyond the sea. Led by their
chief, Shyri, they followed the Esmeraldas River into
the highlands where they defeated the Quitos, a small,
weak Indian tribe. Around A. D. 980 near the borders
of Chimborazo Province, they were confronted by the
strong Puruhá tribe. Unable to defeat the latter,
Shyri married his daughter, Toa, to Duchicela, the
Puruhá Crown Prince, thereby establishing a powerful
kingdom around A. D. 1300. This kingdom was destroyed
by the Incas in 1487. The last king, Cacha Duchicela
Shyri, married his daughter, Paccha, to the Emperor,

Huayna Cápac.   Their son, Atahualpa, was the last
Inca Emperor.   The Caras were ancestors of the
present-day Otavalo Indians, who inhabit the Valley of
Otavalo, and are the most wealthy and independent
native group.

CARBO Y NOBOA, PEDRO JOSE.   Born, March 19, 1813,
Guayaquil.   Died, December 24, 1895, Guayaquil.
Statesman.   One of the most notable public figures of
Ecuador in the 19th century; secretary to the minis-
ter of Foreign Relations, 1835; secretary of the Ecua-
dorean legation to the government of New Granada and
Peru; minister of the Treasury, 1876; supreme chief
of the Province of Guayaquil, 1883.

CARCHI.   Province in northern Ecuador bordering with
Colombia.   Much of the province's 1581 square miles
lie in the Andes, and its Indian inhabitants live from
agriculture and livestock.   The capital, Tulcán, has
an altitude of 9000 feet.   Population (1968 est.),
112, 500.

CARIGUAIRAZO.   Volcano, companion of Chimborazo, which
erupted violently on July 19, 1698, and covered the
surroundings of Ambato and Latacunga with mud and
water with great loss of life in the accompanying
earthquake.

CARONDELET, LUIS FRANCISCO HECTOR, BARON DE.
Born, 1748, at Noyelles, France.   Died, Quito,
August 10, 1807.   Soldier and administrator.   He was
early in the militia and sent to Pensacola, Florida,
where he fought in the Battle of Pensacola in 1763
against the French.   He was named governor of San
Salvador, 1788-1792; governor of Louisiana, 1792-
1797; president of the Audiencia of Quito, 1798-1807.
He built the highway from Quito to Guayaquil and en-
couraged scientific expeditions and explorations.

CARRERA ANDRADE, JORGE.   Born, September 18, 1903,
Quito.   Poet, diplomat.   Co-founder of the Socialist
Party of Ecuador and the unsuccessful Agrarian Party;
consul in various cities in Peru, United States, France,
Japan, Venezuela; senator from Pichincha Province;
ambassador to the United Kingdom (1947); ambassador-
at-large (1960); ambassador to Venezuela (1961),
ambassador to France (1965).   An Ecuadorean poet

of international acclaim whose numerous works have
been translated into several languages. Most important
works: Estanque inefable, 1922; La guirnalda del
silencio, 1926; Boletínes de mar y tierra, 1930;
Latitudes, viajes, hombres, lecturas, 1934; La hora
de las ventanas iluminadas, 1957; País secreto; Cemen-
terio marino; Cántico de las columnas; Poesias esco-
gidas, 1945; Edades poéticas, 1922-56.

CARRION, ALEJANDRO see CARRION MORA, MANUEL
ALEJANDRO

CARRION, BENJAMIN see CARRION MORA, MANUEL
BENJAMIN

CARRION, JERONIMO. Born, July 6, 1801, Cariamanga
(Loja Province). Died, May 5, 1873, Cuenca. Politician. Governor, Azuay Province, 1845-47; deputy
from Loja Province, 1845 and 1852; senator from
Loja Province, 1847-49; vice-president of the Republic,
1859; major general of the Chilean Army, 1866. Presidency: elected, age 64, 1865, one term, first president to be elected by direct popular suffrage; overthrown and replaced by his vice-president Pedro José
de Arteta in 1867.

CARRION MORA, MANUEL ALEJANDRO. Born, Loja,
March 11, 1915. Education: LL. D. , University of
Loja. Lawyer, poet, professor. Member of the
Central Council of the Partido Socialista, he has
occupied various posts in the government. He has
published several volumes of poetry under the simplified form of his distinguished family name: Alejandro
Carrión, including Equatorialco, which was also
printed in a bi-lingual English-Spanish edition, under
the title From the Equator, Dudley Fitts and Francis
St. John, Norfolk, Conn. , 1944.

CARRION MORA, MANUEL BENJAMIN. Born, April 20,
1897, Loja. Education: J. D. , Central University of
Quito. Writer, intellectual, politician. Director of
the daily, El Sol. Minister of Public Education; ambassador to Mexico, Chile, Colombia; deputy various
occasions; delegate to UNESCO; president of the Casa
de la Cultura Ecuatoriana (various occasions); member of the Ecuadorean Socialist Party (PSE); vice-
presidential candidate on the left wing Democratic

National Anti-Conservative Union (UDNA) ticket in
1960; author of: El desencanto de Miguel García,
novel, 1929; Atahualpa, 1956; El nuevo relato ecuatoriano, 1958; García Moreno, el santo del patíbulo,
1959.

CARRION VACA, NICOLAS. Literary figure, 18th century,
Quito.

CARTAGENA ACCORD (Acuerdo de Cartagena). An agreement signed by Bolivia, Chile, Colombia, Ecuador,
and Peru at Cartagena, Colombia, May 26, 1969,
whereby these nations, known as the "Andean Group,"
set up a zonal commission at Lima on trade and
development within the framework of the broader Latin
American Free Trade Association (see ALALC), which
was established after the success of the European
Common Market. Because of their lesser development to date, the Andean nations have needed to ap-
proach their problems in a fashion different from that
of the more industrial nations, such as Mexico, Argentina, Brazil and Venezuela.

CARVAJAL, RAFAEL. Born, near Ibarra, 1818. Died,
Lima, 1877. Lawyer, public servant, poet. Minister
of the Interior and Foreign Relations under García
Moreno, also deputy in the National Congress, vice-
president, and president of the Supreme Court of
Justice. His poetry was largely the work of leisure
moments, in the romantic vein.

CASA DE LA CULTURA ECUATORIANA. Autonomous institution with corporation status, established by a decree
of President José María Velasco Ibarra, for general
promotion of all aspects of the national culture, August
9, 1944. Each province has a "nucleus" of the Casa,
and all publish to some extent in varied fields of cultural and scientific endeavor. It is charged with the
protection of the national cultural heritage. Support
comes from a share (3/4 of 1%) of all export taxes
collected in the nation.

CASPICARA (MANUEL CHILLI). The most notable Ecua-
dorean sculptor. Flourished in the 18th century.
Caspicara's works are mostly of a religious nature.
His best known are found in Quito, and in Popayán,
Colombia.

CASTILLO, JOSE ABEL. Born, October 19, 1854, Guayaquil. Newspaper publisher (El Telégrafo, Guayaquil,
founded February 16, 1884), and pioneer aviation en-
thusiast. After pioneer flights he donated his biplane,
Telégrafo I, to the National Aviation Service, and the
first airmail was inaugurated in 1920, November 4,
between Guayaquil and Quito.

CASTILLO CASTILLO, ABEL ROMEO. Born, Guayaquil,
January 22, 1904. Died, 1971, Guayaquil. Ph. D. in
history, University of Madrid. Politician, diplomat,
journalist. Deputy to National Assembly of 1944-45;
ambassador to Guatemala, Costa Rica, Bolivia, and
Uruguay, 1952-61; dean of the School of Philosophy,
University of Guayaquil; director of the School of
Journalism, University of Guayaquil; member of many
learned societies; co-director of the Guayaquil daily,
El Telégrafo.

CASTILLO DE LEVI, MARIA PIEDAD. Born, July 6, 1888,
Guayaquil. Died, March 4, 1962, Guayaquil. Poet,
daughter of José Abel Castillo and Betsabé Castillo.

CAYAMBE. Volcanic peak near Quito. Elevation, 19, 160
feet.

CAYAPA. An Indian tribe inhabiting primarily the lowlands
of northwestern Ecuador (Esmeraldas Province), although some are still to be found along the coast of
Colombia. Their numbers are estimated at 2000.

CEDOC see CONFEDERACION ECUATORIANA ...

CEDULA DE 1802 see ROYAL DECREE OF 1802

CEDULA UNICA. An identification card which must be
obtained by the citizens of voting age, i. e. , all
literate men and women above 18 years of age. The
Cédula Unica was issued first during the interim
presidency of Clemente Yerovi Indaburo (1966). It
replaced a separate identification and voter's registration card. It was hoped that this would greatly facili-
tate the process of registration of citizens as well as
increase the number of voters.

CENDES see next entry

CENTRO DE DESARROLLO (CENDES).   Development Center.
Concerned with industrial development.

CENTRO DE TURISMO.   Tourist Center.   Government
agency in charge of developing tourism.

CENTURIS   see previous entry

CEOSL   see   CONFEDERACION ECUATORIANA DE OR-
GANIZACIONES ...

CEPE   see   CORPORACION ESTATAL PETROLERA
ECUATORIANA

CESCANOON MORALES, IGNACIO.   Born, before 1725,
Cuenca.   Military commander, poet, critic, he served
as royal treasurer in Cuenca, as well as Regidor and
Alcalde Ordinario (similar to city council member and
lower court judge).   Military commander at Guayaquil.
One of the founders of the library at Lima.

CEVALLOS, PEDRO FERMIN.   Born, July 7, 1812, Ambato.
Died, May 21, 1893, Quito.   Historian, lawyer.
Author of Historia del Ecuador in six volumes.   His
Compendio de la Historia del Ecuador was declared
the official school text in 1871.

CEVALLOS GARCIA, GABRIEL.   Born, January 5, 1914,
Cuenca.   Education: J. D. , University of Cuenca.
Historian, educator.   Dean, Faculty of Philosophy,
University of Cuenca, 1941-49; rector, same, 1946-47;
author: Reflexiones sobre la historia del Ecuador,
Vol. I, 1957, Vol. II, 1960; two more volumes in
preparation.

CFP   see   CONCENTRACION DE FUERZAS POPULARES

CHAGRA.   Name given to persons in the highland region
who are not from the capital city, Quito.   The word
also carries the connotation of little culture and taste.

CHAHUARMISHQUE.   The Ecuadorean equivalent of the
Mexican aguamiel, the unfermented juice of the Agave
americana or cabuya.   Usually consumed in the unfermented, aguamiel, form in Ecuador; but in the
fermented form, known as pulque in Mexico.

"CHARTER OF SLAVERY" see CONSTITUTIONS

CHATHAM ISLAND see SAN CRISTOBAL

CHAULLABAMBA. An archeological zone primarily in the
Cuenca basin. The phase dates probably back to as
early as 620 B. C. and is particularly known for its
well-made pottery. Ceramic figurines and stone imple-
ments are rare.

CHAVEZ FRANCO, MODESTO. Born, November 22, 1872,
Santa Rosa, Province of El Oro. Died, May 14, 1952,
Guayaquil. Folklorist and historian. Founder of the
Municipal Library and Museum of Guayaquil. Because
of his writings, he was named "Lifetime Chronicler of
Guayaquil." Principle work: Chronicles of Old Guaya-
quil.

CHECA, FELICIANO. Born, June 8, 1779, Quito. Died,
1846, Quito. Precursor of Ecuador's independence.
Rose to the rank of colonel and fought under Sucre in
the Battle of Pichincha (1822). Military commander
of the cantón of Latacunga.

CHICHA. A beer-like beverage fermented from sprouted
corn. It dates back to pre-Columbian days.

CHICHERIA. Place where chicha is sold.

CHIMBORAZO. Province in the central Ecuadorean highlands. Area, 2322 square miles; population (1968
est.), 345,000.

CHIMBORAZO. The highest mountain peak in the Cordillera
Real, reaching an elevation of 20,577 feet. It is located in the province of the same name and is best
seen from the city of Riobamba. The German naturalist, Baron Alexander von Humboldt, established an
altitude record for his time when he ascended Chimborazo to an elevation of 19,390 feet in 1802. The
summit was reached by Edward Whymper in 1880.

CHINCHONA see CINCHONA

CHIRIBOGA NAVARRO, ANGEL ISAAC. Born, August 2,
1889, Quito. Died, 1960, Quito. Educated at the
Central University of Quito and the War Academy

Soldier. Diplomat. Historian. Besides serving in
various diplomatic posts, including Brussels with the
rank of ambassador, General Chiriboga was once minister of Foreign Affairs, and author of the Historia
General Militar del Ecuador. He was commanding
general of the sector of the army which attacked Quito
in the "Four Days' War" in 1932, and prevented
Neftalí Bonifaz Ascásubi from taking office as President.

CHOCLO. Green corn, roasting ear, corn-on-the-cob.

CHOCLOTANDA. Tamal made of green corn cut from the
cob and ground to a paste to which various condiments
are added with meat, if available. Corn husks are
used as wrappers and cooking is in a steam bath.

CHOLO. The somewhat pejorative name given to Indians
who have become Europeanized. The feminine form,
chola, has the same connotation, but in Cuenca it
becomes a rather affectionate term with overtones of
eroticism and attraction.

CHONTA. A very hard wood from a palm of the same
name (Bactris sp.). Also a folk-dance of the yumbos
(q. v.).

CHORRERA. An archeological zone the sites of which are
along the Guayas coast from the Santa Elena Península
northward to the Palmer region and along the banks of
the Daule and Babahoyo rivers. It dates back to 850
B. C. and is the first archeological phase in Ecuador
where the sites are not restricted to the shore.

CHULLA. A person of either sex who does not belong to
the upper class but who by virtue of his education,
clothing, bearing, and ambitions may pass for a member of that class. The Quechua word means careless
or worthless.

CHULLALEVA. Equivalent of chulla, said to come from the
Quechua meaning one who is worth only the coat
(levita) on his back.

CHUYA. Clear, without residue, said of beverage; also,
diluted with water, watered.

CID   see   COALICION INSTITUCIONALISTA DEMOCRATICA

LA CIENAGA, "PEACE OF." Treaty signed at the Hacienda of La Ciénaga, February 7, 1831, whereby Ecuador's separation from Gran Colombia was recognized.

CIEZA DE LEON, PEDRO DE. Born, ca. 1522, Sevilla. Died, July 1554, Sevilla. Historian, military leader. His Chronicle of Perú is considered perhaps the most important single contemporary history of the Conquest and is important for Ecuadorean as well as Peruvian history.

CINCHONA BARK (chinchona). Source of the drug quinine, which enabled the control and cure of malaria. An important Ecuadorean export for many years, it comes from the bark of several trees of the area, especially Cinchona ledgeriana and C. succirubra. Named for the Count Chinchón, Luis Jerónimo Fernández de Cabrera, Bovadilla y Mendoza (1608-1647), young nobleman, recently married, who was named viceroy of Peru, or for his wife, who contracted malaria, and traditionally was the first European known to have been cured by use of the infusions from the bark. Also called Peruvian bark.

CNT   see   COMISION NACIONAL DEL TRIGO

COALICION INSTITUCIONALISTA DEMOCRATICA (CID). A center-right political party founded on February 20, 1965 by Otto Arosemena Gómez. The party elected one member each to the Chamber of Deputies and Senate in 1968. It has, so far, supported the conservatives.

COBA ROBALINO, JOSE MARIA. Born, September 9, 1880, Píllaro. Died, June 16, 1935. Historian and folklorist. His writings on the local history and customs of his native area are considered highly accurate examples of early folklore studies in Ecuador.

COE   see   CONFEDERACION OBRERA ECUATORIANA

COFAN. An Indian tribe living in the northwestern-most part of Ecuador's Oriente. They number around 400 and have not been hostile in their contacts with the Europeanized population.

COFIEC see COMPAÑIA ECUATORIANA DE DESARROLLO

COLEGIO DE LA PROVIDENCIA.   One of several church-operated schools for girls in Quito.

COLEGIO DE SAN ANDRES.   The first school established in the Ecuadorean area for the education of the natives, 1535.   See RICKE, FRAY JODOCO.

COLEGIO MILITAR.   The Military College, located in Quito, was founded in 1899.   It profoundly changed the character of the military because it allowed those set on a military career to achieve rank in an institution of higher learning in addition to accomplishment on the battlefield.

COLON, ISLAS DE see GALAPAGOS

COLORADO.   An Indian tribe, now much diminished in numbers, centering on the western slope of the Andes in Pichincha Province, around Santo Domingo.   So called because of the red dye from the achiote with which they plaster their hair until it looks like a casque or helmet.

COMERCIO, EL.   Second largest newspaper in Ecuador with a daily circulation of about 70,000.   It was first published in Quito on January 1, 1906.   Its editorial policy is independent-liberal.

COMISION DE VALORES see CV-CFN

COMISION NACIONAL DEL TRIGO (CNT).   National Wheat Commission.

COMPAÑIA DEL FERROCARRIL DEL SUR.   The original name given to the Guayaquil and Quito Railroad.

COMPAÑIA ECUATORIANA DE DESARROLLO (COFIEC).   Ecuadorean Development Company, a private finance corporation founded in 1966.

COMPAÑIAS ORGANICAS NACIONALES DE OFENSIVA REVOLUCIONARIA (CONDOR).   A political movement organized in February 1941 by seven students of the Central University of Quito.   The movement was intended to save the country from the international

disaster of 1941 in which Ecuador suffered a military
defeat by Peru. The name of the movement was
changed a year later to the present-day Acción Revolucionaria Nacionalista Ecuatoriana (ARNE).

COMUNA. Commune; under the 1937 law, an autonomous
political unit permitted to the Indian settlements, presided over by an elective council (cabildo) of five with
a president as head.

CONCENTRACION DE FUERZAS POPULARES (CFP). A
personalistic political party which originated as a
splinter group from admirers of José María Velasco
Ibarra on March 30, 1946. It was organized by Carlos
Guevara Moreno and its strength is concentrated in
the coastal city of Guayaquil. The zenith of party
strength was reached in 1956 presidential election when
Guevara Moreno was third with 24 percent of the valid
votes cast. The party has since split into two factions:
the major portion follows Asaad Bucaram, twice mayor
of Guayaquil; the minor faction is led by Hanna Musse
and is also concentrated in Guayaquil. In the 1968
presidential election, the Bucaram faction supported
the liberal FID coalition while the other sided with
Velasco Ibarra. The CFP, both factions together,
elected three deputies to the 1968 legislature.

CONCERTAJE. A form of debt peonage to which the Indian
population was subjected after the mita was outlawed.
Abolished by President Baquerizo Moreno in 1918.

CONCORDAT OF 1862. An agreement signed by the Vatican
and President Gabriel García Moreno under which
temporal rule, as represented in the Ecuadorean State,
was officially subordinate to the Vicar of Christ's
authority. A short time later (1872) the country was
dedicated to the Sacred Heart of Jesús and, shortly
afterwards, to the Immaculate Conception. Under the
Concordat the patronato was abrogated and the church
was granted control of publication and importation of
books. Roman Catholicism also became the sole and
exclusive religion of the Republic. Church and state
were officially separated under the 1906 Constitution,
thereby finally revoking the Concordat.

CONDAMINE, CHARLES MARIE DE LA. Born, January
28, 1701, Paris. Died, February 4, 1774, Paris.

French scientist, member of the expedition sent by
Louis XV to perform experiments and surveys, including the measurement of one degree of the arc of
the earth's circumference at the equator from which
the length of the meter was determined (1735-43).
Author: Relation abrégée d'un voyage fait dans l'in-
terieur de l'Amérique meridionale, 1745; Mésure des
trois degrés du méridien dans l'hemisphére austral,
1751; Histoire des pyramides de Quito, 1751.

CONDUMIO. Filling or stuffing in various types of breads
and pastries.

CONFEDERACION DE TRABAJADORES ECUATORIANOS
(CTE). Organized in 1944. Largest labor confederation in Ecuador. Initially controlled by the socialists,
it was led for a long time by the communists. At
present, the secretary general of the Federation is
Telmo Hidalgo, a radical-socialist. The Communists,
however, still exercise major control and the Federation continues to be affiliated with the Communist World
Federation of Trade Unions. The largest portion of
CTE membership comes from the coastal provinces.

CONFEDERACION ECUATORIANA DE OBREROS CATOLICOS
(CEDOC). The oldest labor confederation in Ecuador
dating back to 1938. CEDOC is affiliated with the
International Confederation of Free Trade Unions
(ICFTU). The Confederation is conservative in orientation but claims not to support any of the existing
conservative parties. Most of its membership comes
from the highland region.

CONFEDERACION ECUATORIANA DE ORGANIZACIONES DE
SINDICATOS LIBRES (CEOSL). Second largest of the
Ecuadorean labor groups, affiliated with the ORIT
(Interamerican Organization of Workers)--an AFL/CIO
extension activity in labor union organization and activity.

CONFEDERACION OBRERA ECUATORIANA (COE). Ecuadorean Workers' Confederation, a now defunct labor
union organized in 1897. Conservative in ideology, it
recruited its members primarily from among Guayaquil's citizens.

CONFERENCE OF GUAYAQUIL. On July 26-27, 1822, at
Guayaquil, Simón Bolívar, Liberator of New Granada,

and José de San Martín (1778-1850), winner of Argen-
tine and Chile Independence (and from 1820 named
Protector of Peru), met at a spot now marked by an
imposing monument on the edge of the harbor of
Guayaquil. No accurate knowledge of what occurred
is known to the present time, but immediately thereafter San Martín resigned his command in Peru, and
journeyed back to the South whence he had come,
leaving Bolívar to complete the defeat of the Spanish
at the Battles of Junín and Ayacucho, both in Peru,
two years later.

CONSTANTE, THEO. Born in 1934, Guayaquil. Educated
at the School of Fine Arts, Guayaquil. Contemporary
Ecuadorean painter.

CONSTITUENT CONVENTION. Term used in Ecuadorean
politics (convención constituyente) to describe a political body especially established either to draft a
new constitution or to revise an old one, and often
to choose a new president.

CONSTITUTIONS. Ecuador's present (1972) constitution,
effective as of May 25, 1967, is the sixteenth since
the country's separation from Gran Colombia in 1830.
Excluded is the short-lived 1938 Constitution never
officially promulgated. Some of the constitutions have
had a large impact on the political process because of
their introduction of extremist or unique features.
The 1843 Constitution introduced by Juan José Flores
is also known as the "Charter of Slavery" because of
its suppressive measures. The 1869 Constitution introduced by Gabriel García Moreno is also known as the
"Black Charter" because, among other things, it provided that only practicing Catholics could become citizens. Unique or novel for Ecuador may be considered
the constitutions of 1861, 1897, 1906, and 1929. The
1861 Constitution provided for the first time for direct
popular suffrage. The 1897 Constitution provided for
respect of religious minorities and abolition of the
death penalty. The 1906 Constitution provided for the
separation of church and state. Finally, the 1929
Constitution gave women the right to vote, the first
in Latin America to do so. There are a number of
characteristics shared by the Ecuadorean constitutions.
The formal structure of government has remained
intact throughout the entire republican period. All

constitutions, except that of 1830, refer to the nation as a republic. All, furthermore, provide for a chief executive to be called a president, for unitary structure, and for a functional division of power between the executive, legislative, and judicial branches of government. The majority (11) of the constitutions also provide for a representative and democratic state. While this represents a general agreement concerning the exercise of sovereignty, it has been frequently disputed and has reflected the radicall-liberal or conservative domination of government. Thus, eight constitutions, that of 1946 being the latest, state that sovereignty originates with God; six constitutions, the first being that of 1878, place the origin of sovereignty with the people or the nation, while two make no mention of this. For a chronological listing of Ecuador's constitutions, see Appendix 6.

CONVIO-CANASEAL, DIEGO DE. Died, Quito. Public official. President of the Audiencia of Quito, 1670-73.

CORAL, LUCIANO. Born, in Carchi. Died, January 28, 1912, Quito. Journalist, author, politician. Founder of several journals of political satire. After the 1895 revolution he became Eloy Alfaro's private secretary; governor of Carchi; deputy from Imbabura Province. Founder of the Guayaquil daily El Tiempo in 1899 and the Quito daily El Tiempo in 1901. Died with Eloy Alfaro by mob action.

CORDERO CRESPO, LUIS. Born, April 6, 1833, Surampalti (Cañar Province). Died, January 30, 1912, Cuenca. Education: J.D., University of Quito. Author, politician, lawyer. Political chief of Cuenca, 1876; member of the Provisional Junta, July 9, 1883 to February 9, 1884; senator from Azuay Province and president of the Senate, 1885; senator from the provinces of Bolívar and Azuay, 1892; minister in Chile, 1910; rector of the University of Azuay, 1911. Presidency: elected (popular), age 59, 1892, one term, resigned after a liberal uprising and was succeeded by his Vice-president Vicente Lucio Salazar, in 1895. As a lifelong student of the Quechua language, he compiled a Diccionario quichua, translated prose and poetry into the language, and did comparative studies of the dialects. He was also an able amateur botanist. See Bibliography.

CORDILLERA REAL. The western Andean Cordillera.
Quito, Ambato, Riobamba, and other cities of the
Sierra lie between this and the Cordillera Oriental in
the great intervening valley.

CORDOBA, JOSE MARIA. Born, in Río Negro, Colombia,
September 8, 1799. Died, Santuario, October 17, 1829.
Engineer and military leader. He studied under Dr.
Francisco José de Caldas at Popayán, but at the age
of 15 entered the insurgent army against Spanish rule.
Veteran of many battles, he ascended rapidly to become a general. His Bogotá Batallón was important
in the battle of Pichincha, May 24, 1822, which brought
Ecuador into the Free area of New Granada (Gran
Colombia). He fought also at Ayacucho, victoriously,
and received all the decorations at the disposal of
Bolívar and Sucre. Córdoba was Bolívar's minister
of war, but later rebelled against the "Liberator,"
was cornered at the head of a force of 300 men, by
3000 under O'Leary, and murdered.

CORDOVA NIETO, ANDRES. Born, May 8, 1892, Cañar.
Education: J.D., University of Azuay (Cuenca), 1919.
Lawyer, politician. Deputy from Azuay Province,
1922-25, 1934-35, 1939-40; professor of civil law,
University of Azuay, 1925-43; dean of that university,
1939-43; senator from Azuay Province, 1930-31; member of Constituent Convention, 1967; unsuccessful
presidential candidate of the center-left FID coalition
in the 1968 election. Presidency: non-elected, age
47, 1939; replaced interim president Carlos Alberto
Arroyo del Río, who resigned in order to run in the
1940 presidential election.

CORDOVA RIVERA, GONZALO S. Born, July 15, 1863,
Cuenca. Died, April 13, 1928, Valparaíso, Chile.
Education: J.D., University of Cuenca. Lawyer,
politician. Deputy from Cañar Province, 1892-97;
governor of Cañar, 1898-1902; minister of Interior,
1903-1906; senator from Carchi Province and vice-
president of the Senate, 1912; minister to Chile, Argentina, and the United States, 1911-13; minister to
Venezuela, 1922. Presidency: elected (popular),
age 61, 1924, one term, overthrown by revolution in
1925.

CORPORACION ESTATAL PETROLERA ECUATORIANA
(CEPE). The Ecuadorian State Petroleum Corporation, established October 22, 1971, to supervise all
aspects of exploitation of oil resources, including
foreign investments and operations.

CORPORACION FINANCIERA NACIONAL see CV-CFN

CORRAL, MIGUEL ANGEL. Born, Cuenca, 1833. Died,
Quito, May 3, 1883. Lawyer, poet, distinguished
public servant, editor of the official gazette, Supreme
Court minister. Corral is regarded as perhaps the
most talented poet of the 19th century in Ecuador.

COSTA. The coastal lowlands 12 to 100 miles wide, which
cover slightly more than 26,000 square miles, or
about one-fourth of Ecuador's national territory.
Politically, the Costa is divided into five provinces:
El Oro, Esmeraldas, Guayas, Los Ríos and Manabí.

COSTEÑO. A person living in or native of the lowlands
(Costa).

COTOPAXI. Province in the Central highland of Ecuador,
formerly known as the Province of León. Area 2241
square miles. Population (1968 est.), 225,000.

COTOPAXI. Probably the highest active volcano in the
world, rising to a height of 19,347 feet. It is in the
province of the same name and about 35 miles south
of Quito. First ascended in 1872.

CRESPO TORAL, REMIGIO. Born, August 4, 1860, Cuenca.
Died, July 8, 1939, Cuenca. Man of letters, diplomat, poet. President of the National Congress, 1888;
rector, University of Cuenca. One of the most important literary figures not only of Ecuador, but of
all South America. Wrote on history, economics,
sociology, and literature.

CRIOLLO. Term used in Spanish to denote a person of
pure Spanish blood, but born in the Western Hemisphere. It often takes on a nationalistic connotation,
or is used to indicate non-Indian influence or origin.

CTE see CONFEDERACION DE TRABAJADORES ECUA-
TORIANOS

CUADRA, JOSE DE LA. Born, September 3, 1903, Guayaquil. Died, February 26, 1941, Guayaquil. Education:
J. D., University of Guayaquil. Educator, novelist.
Secretary general of Public Administration; consul in
Argentina and Uruguay. One of the most important
20th-century Ecuadorean novelists. Member of the
"Grupo de Guayaquil." Important works: Los san-
gurimas, 1934; El montuvio ecuatoriano, 1937; Horno,
1932; Guasintón, 1938.

CUENCA. Capital of the Province of Azuay. Third largest
city of Ecuador. Population (1968 est.), 100,000.
Founded in 1557 by Gil Ramírez Dávalos and Fr.
Vicente Solano.

CUERO Y CAICEDO, JOSE. Born, Popayán, Colombia.
Died, 1815, Lima, Peru. Education: doctor of
theology, University of Saint Thomas Aquinas (Quito).
Precursor of Ecuador's Independence; Bishop of Cuenca,
Popayán and Quito (1806); president of the 1809 patri-
otic junta, formed in the house of Manuela Cañizares.

CUEVA, MARIANO. Born, August 5, 1810, Cuenca. Died,
March 18, 1882. Education: J. D., Central University
of Quito, 1831. Lawyer, politician, journalist. Deputy
from Azuay Province to the 1852 Constituent Assembly;
minister of the Supreme Court; governor of Azuay
Province; deputy to the 1878 Convention and senator,
1872, representing Azuay Province; founder of the
newspapers, El Cuencano, La República, and El
Atalaya.

CUEVA TAMARIZ, CARLOS. Born, November 5, 1898,
Cuenca. Education: J. D., University of Cuenca,
1922. Educator, lawyer, politician. Minister of
Public Education; rector of the University of Cuenca;
major leader of the Ecuadorean Socialist Party; vice-
presidential candidate on the 1948 Socialist ticket;
secretary general of the United Socialist Party, 1966-
69.

CURUCHUPA. Pejorative expression applied to the conservatives in politics, suggesting their subservience to
the church.

CUTAMA RUMI. Quechua for large grinding stone, equivalent to the Mexican "metate." The smaller stone

used with it is the "gua-gua rumi" or "mano" in
Spanish.

CUTU. Name applied by the Quechua-speaking populace to
those who accept at least partially the customs and
traits of their superiors in the social strata. Derived from "cotona" the name given to the simple
collarless (and sometimes sleeveless) shirt or garment
which Europeans provided the native population to
cover their nakedness.

CV-CFN. Comisión de Valores - Corporación Financiera
Nacional: National Securities Commission - National
Finance Corporation. Government agency founded in
1964. Provides credit to larger industries.

- D -

DAQUILEMA, FERNANDO. Died, April 8, 1870, Yaruquíes,
Chimborazo. So-called "King of Cacha, " he was the
(messianic) leader of an Indian uprising.

DARWIN, CHARLES ROBERT. Born, February 12, 1809,
Shrewsbury, England. Died, April 19, 1882, London.
British naturalist, author of Origin of Species, which
was in part based on studies made on the Galápagos
Islands during the 1835 expedition of HMS Beagle to
South America. The UNESCO Wildlife Conservation
Station on the Island of Santa Cruz in the Galápagos
is named for him.

DAULE see TEJAR

DAULE RIVER. Principal tributary of the Guayas river.
They join just above the city of Guayaquil.

DAVILA ANDRADE, CESAR. Born, 1918, Cuenca. Died,
May 2, 1967, Caracas, Venezuela. Writer and poet.
Author: Especie me has vencido, 1946; Catedral
salvaje, 1951; Trece relatos, 1955; Arco de instantes
(poems), 1959.

DECEPCION. In Ecuador the word takes on a meaning
exactly opposite to its obvious English cognate and
means "disenchantment. "

DECEPCIONARSE.   To become disenchanted with, to un-
deceive one's self.

DECIDOR.   Flatterer.

DEFORNO   see   DESARROLLO FORESTAL NOROCCIDENTAL

DESAGUAR.   To place vegetables or other edibles in water
for the purpose of removing an undesirable flavor or
harmful substance.

DESARROLLO FORESTAL NOROCCIDENTAL (DEFORNO).
A joint Ecuadorean-FAO project founded in 1967.
Under this project a forest resource inventory is
being conducted to establish the different varieties of
trees growing in the country and the extent of the respective stands.

DESEMBUCHAR.   To tell someone what one thinks of him,
give someone a piece of one's mind.

DESMEDIDO.   Not only "unrestrained" as classically, but
"obstinate, " "indolent, " "unwilling to perform small
tasks. "

DESPENARSE.   To die after a long and painful illness.

DIAZ CUEVA, MIGUEL.   Born, April 17, 1919, Cuenca.
Education: J. D. , University of Cuenca.   Educator,
bibliographer-historian.   Director of the National
Archives of History (Azuay Province) 1964.   Author:
Bibliografía de Honorato Vásquez, 1955; Bibliografía
de Fray Vicente Solano, 1965; Bibliografía de Manuel
J. Calle (1969).

DIAZ DE ARMENDARIZ, LOPE (Marqués de Cadereyta).
Born, ca. 1575, Quito, son of President of the Audiencia Lope Aux Díez de Armendáriz (q. v. , under AUX).
Education: Royal College in Madrid.   Diplomat, politician.   Mayordomo of Queen Isabel; general of the
West Indian Fleet (Galeones de las Indias); Spanish
ambassador to the German Court; viceroy of Mexico,
September 16, 1635 to August 27, 1640.   Responsible
for the construction of the Great Drainage Canal from
Lake Texcoco during his term as Viceroy.   His last
name appears also as Díez de Aux de Armendáriz.

DIAZ DE PINEDA, GONZALO. Died, 1544. Captain-general of Quito, associate of Benalcázar. In 1539 he founded the Asiento [outpost] de Sevilla de Oro, now Macas, on the eastern side of the Andes. Explorer under Gonzalo Pizarro, he participated in the revolt against the New Laws, whereby Spain tried to restore to the Indians part of what they had lost in the conquest, and to recognize their rights as human beings. Forced to flee to the Sierra, he died there.

DIEZ DE AUX DE ARMENDARIZ see DIAZ DE ARMENDARIZ

DIGUJA, JOSE. Born, Castilla la Vieja. Military officer, public official. Colonel in the Royal Spanish Army; president of the Audiencia of Quito, July 1767 to late 1768.

DIRECCION NACIONAL DEL BANANO. National Banana Directorate. The bureau supervises the processing of bananas and their shipment abroad.

DNB see previous entry

DOLIENTE. A mourner at a funeral.

- E -

EDUCATION. European education practices had their beginnings in Ecuador early in the colonial period when church orders began to operate schools for the teaching of arts and crafts to a picked few of the indigenous population. Only a limited number were taught to read and write Spanish as well as to perform their labors as skilled artisans. Growth in the European population brought the demand for more educational facilities, but primary schooling was for the most part given in the home by tutors or relatives. Secondary schooling was gradually begun in seminary-type colegios, operated chiefly for the training of new members for the religious orders, so that their orientation was towards theology, philosophy, and canon law, as in all European schools of the time. Very few schools were operated by nonreligious personnel until after independence. Simón Bolívar and others in the early period after separation from Spain proposed public schools, and some 20 were set up in Ecuador. When Gran Colombia fell apart, however, conditions in Ecuador became so chaotic that it was not until the time of García Moreno, 1860-1875, that any formal planning of an educational system was undertaken or put into effect. The general educational system was at that time developed, at all levels, still officially under the control and aegis of the Roman Catholic Church, including an enlarged university system. In 1906 with abrogation of the Concordat, teaching by laymen was legalized. See also: SCHOOLS; UNIVERSITIES.

EGAS, CAMILO. Born, December 10, 1895, Quito. Died, 1962, New York. Educated in the School of Fine Arts, Quito; Royal Chalcography and Institute of Fine Arts, Rome; San Fernando Institute, Madrid. Painter and professor of fine arts, Quito. Artistic director, Sucre National Theater, Quito. Instructor in painting in the New York School of Social Research. Winner of many medals, his work was widely exhibited in Ecuador, Italy, France, and New York, and is included in numerous collections.

EGAS MIRANDA, JOSE MARIA. Born, 1893? Manta. Educated at Guayaquil. J.D., licenciate in social sciences. Lawyer, poet, professor, judge. Member of the Supreme Court of Ecuador and of the Electoral Tribunal. He has been the recipient of much international cultural recognition. He is the last surviving member of the Modernist group in his country, which included Arturo Borja, Ernesto Noboa Caamaño, Humberto Fierro, José A. Falconi Villagómez, Medardo Angel Silva, and José María Egas himself.

EGAS MIRANDA, MIGUEL AUGUSTO. Born, 1895, Manta. Poet, resident of Guayaquil since childhood. Leader in the Vanguardist Movement in poetry, introducing the various European currents to Ecuador, but essentially a nativist with originality and vitality. His work has been included in a number of anthologies, and in two volumes under his own name.

ELAN. The name adopted by a group of poets which included Alejandro Carrión, José Alfredo Llerena, Jorge Fernández, Augusto Sacoto Arias, and others.

ELIZALDE Y LA MAR, ANTONIO DE. Born, 1795; died,
1862. Governing official of the late Spanish period.
Liberal and wealthy in his own right, he contributed
to the independence movement at Guayaquil from 1820,
became a leader of the military forces then, and
again in 1845 when he opposed the conservatism of
General Juan José Flores. Supported the Roca-Noboa-
Olmedo triumvirate (qq. v.), as supreme chief of
army, yielding to Noboa's claims to the presidency.
Thereafter active in diplomacy of boundary negotiations with Peru and Colombia.

EL ORO. Southernmost province of coastal Ecuador.
Area, 3053 square miles; population (1968 est.),
212, 000.

"ELOY ALFARO" MILITARY AERONAUTICAL SCHOOL.
The Ecuadorean national military air academy.

EL SOL. Newspaper founded January 21, 1951 by Manuel
Benjamín Carrión Mora, more usually known by his
simplified name, Benjamín Carrión, the leftist politician and writer.

EMBROMAR. To be slow to pay one's debts.

EMPAÑETAR. To plaster a house or wall, or to apply the
mud to a wattle construction.

EMPINGOROTARSE. To dress in a conspicuous or unusual
fashion.

EMPONZOÑADO. Angry, vengeful, ill-humored.

EMPRETECER(SE). To paint black, to turn black or dis-
colored.

ENCOGIDO. Indian who withdraws within himself and keeps
to a place in the lower levels of society.

ENRIQUEZ GALLO, ALBERTO. Born, July 24, 1895,
Tanicuchi (León Province). Died, July 13, 1962,
Quito. Education: Colegio Militar "Eloy Alfaro,"
Quito, 1912. Soldier. He rose to the rank of general, 1937; minister of Defense, 1935; unsuccessful
presidential candidate of a liberal socialist coalition
in 1948. Presidency: non-elected, age 42, 1937;

took over from Federico Páez, who resigned; abdicated in favor of Manuel María Borrero after having convoked the Constituent Convention of 1938.

ENTRON.   Indian who is not on the upward swing in the social movement and pushes in where he is not wanted, i. e. a deprecatory term which corresponds to "social climber."

ESCOBEDO, GREGORIO.   Spanish officer at Guayaquil at the time of the October 5, 1820, Declaration of Independence, at which time he joined the insurgency and was named president of the Provisional Council.   He devoted his efforts to the military campaign against Spain.

ESCOBILLAR.   Student slang, to solicit favor by flattery or obsequious behavior; "to polish the apple." (Literally, to sweep with a whisk broom.)

ESCUCHON.   Eavesdropper.

ESCUDERO, GONZALO.   Born, September 28, 1903, Quito. Education, J. D. , Universidad Central, Quito.   Professor, lawyer, poet, diplomat.   Deputy, Constituent Assembly, 1928-30; senator for press and cultural institutions, 1931; diplomatic posts in Paris, Panamá, Buenos Aires, Washington, Mexico, and in many international conferences.

ESCUELA NACIONAL DE BELLAS ARTES.   The National School of Fine Arts in Quito, founded in May 1872 by order of President García Moreno and under the direction of Luis Cadena, who had just returned from his studies in Italy.   It has continued to function through many vicissitudes as the principal and oftentimes only government-supported center for instruction in the plastic arts, and agency for the preservation of national art treasures.

ESMERALDAS.   An Indian tribe that received its name from the emeralds which were found in their territory by the Spanish Conquerors.   Their aboriginal name is uncertain.

ESMERALDAS.   Capital of the Province of Esmeraldas. Population (1968 est.), 55, 000.   With the completion

of the oil pipe line from the Lago Agrio fields east
of the Andes, Esmeraldas has become the chief oil
export center for Ecuador.

ESMERALDAS. The northernmost province of the Ecuadorean coast. Area, 5680 square miles; population (1968
est.), 159,100.

ESMERALDAS RIVER. One of the major rivers of Ecuador.
Along with its tributaries it plays a significant role
(next only to the Guayas river system) in inland traf-
fic and transport.

ESPEJO, EUGENIO see SANTA CRUZ Y ESPEJO,
FRANCISCO JAVIER EUGENIO DE

ESPINEL CEDEÑO, ILEANA. Born, October 31, 1933.
Education: bachelor in modern humanities, Religious
School of Mary the Helper, and student at the School
of Philosophy and Letters of the University of Guayaquil. Poet, feminist, writer. Author of various
volumes of poetry, published in Ecuador and abroad.
Her poetry has been translated into English, French,
Italian, and Greek. Member of the "Club of Poetry, "
writer for the cultural pages of newspapers in Mexico,
Ecuador, Venezuela. Served from 1967 to 1970 as
member of City Council of Guayaquil. Her poetry
has attracted students and critics, including Rigoberto
Cordero y León in a study titled, Eleana Espinel,
alma estelar.

ESPINOSA POLIT, AURELIO. Born, July 11, 1894, Quito.
Died, January 21, 1961, Quito. Education: Compañía
de Jesús (Society of Jesus), studied in England,
France and Italy. Clergyman, poet, author, translator, historian, founder of many schools. Translator
of Latin and English books into Spanish. Renowned
poet and critic.

ESPINOZA, JUAN JAVIER. Born, January 20, 1815, Quito.
Died, September 4, 1870, Quito. Education: J. D. ,
University of Quito, 1838. Lawyer, politician; consul
in Lima, 1849; district attorney of the Supreme Court,
1865. Presidency: elected (popular), age 53, 1868,
one term; overthrown by Gabriel García Moreno in
1869.

ESPINOZA-BONIFAZ ARBITRATION CONVENTION. August
1, 1887. Provided that Ecuador and Peru submit
their questions of boundaries to the King of Spain.
The latter would act as arbiter and his decision would
be binding on both nations without appeal. In case the
King of Spain refused to act as arbiter, the President
of France, the King of Belgium, and the Council of
the Swiss Federation, in the order named, were to be
asked to serve. The two countries had to present
their case before the arbiter within a year of his acceptance. Named for José Modesto Espinoza, Ecuadorean minister of Foreign Relations, and Emilio
Bonifaz, Peruvian ambassador plenipotentiary.

ESTACADOR. Said of a horse which is given to sudden
stops or to the refusal to follow a given route.

ESTACARSE. Of horses, to balk or to stop suddenly; to
take a firm stand.

ESTANTE. Name given to the posts or columns used as
supports for houses constructed on the coastal flood
plains to raise them above high water level and keep
them from dampness and vermin.

ESTETE, MIGUEL DE. Born, Santo Domingo de la Calzada,
Rioja, Spain. Died, place and date unknown. Con-
quistador. Went to Peru about 1537. Estete fought
under Francisco de Pizarro at Cajamarca when
Atahualpa was captured, shared in the booty, then
returned to Peru where he was one of the founders
of Huamanga in 1553. He wrote a Notice on Peru,
describing the conquest, an important early source
on Ecuadorean history.

ESTRADA, EMILIO. Born, May 28, 1855, Quito. Died,
December 21, 1911, Guayaquil. Education: Colegio
Rocafuerte, Guayaquil, 1869. Industrialist, politician.
Governor of Guayas Province, 1895, 1909 and 1910;
vice-president of the Chamber of Deputies, 1899-1900;
"fiscal inspector of consulates," 1906. Presidency:
elected (popular), age 56, 1911, one term; died in
office the same year.

EVIA, JACINTO DE. Born, 1620, Guayaquil. Teacher
and poet. His works were published in 1675 in
Madrid.

- F -

FACHALINA. <u>Mantilla</u> or cloth pieces used to cover the head.

FACHENDOSO. Ostentatious.

FAITE. Quarrelsome individual, "strutter."

FARFAN, ANTONIO. Born, Cuzco, about 1795. Died, Cuenca, date not found. Military leader who achieved the rank of general in the wars for independence. He was wounded in the Battle of Yaguachi, September 17, 1821, and led the Guayaquil Grenadiers at the Battle of Pichincha, May 24, 1822. After independence was attained he remained in Ecuador, where he became an active supporter of Flores in the separatist movement, and later led the forces which put down the dissensions of 1833-34.

FDN see FRENTE DEMOCRATICO NACIONAL

FEBRES CORDERO, LEON DE. Born, 1797, Maracaibo, Venezuela. Died, 1872, Guayaquil. Military leader. He began as a soldier in the Spanish army in Venezuela when he was 15. Sent to Peru with an elite regiment, he lost favor because of his ideas on administrative reform. Recalled to Venezuela, he was then sent to Guayaquil, where he joined the revolutionary movement in the Ecuadorean area, under Bolívar, Sucre, and San Martín. Febrés Cordero fought at the Battle of Pichincha and in the war with Perú in 1828. He led in the 1830 separatist action of Ecuador from Gran Colombia.

FEBRES CORDERO MUÑOZ, FRANCISCO (HERMANO MIGUEL). Born, November 7, 1854, Cuenca. Died, February 9, 1910, Premiá de Mar, Spain. Member of the La Salle Order. Writer, educator, highly respected and honored in his country.

FEDERACION DE ESTUDIANTES UNIVERSITARIOS DEL ECUADOR (FEUE). Organized in 1944. A student association which has branches in every Ecuadorean university. Its leaders have in the last decade been leftists ranging from Castroites to Maoists and sometimes revolutionary socialists. The FEUE has participated since its inception in practically every extra-legal change of government with the exception of the overthrow of President José María Velasco Ibarra by Colonel Carlos Mancheno in 1947. It has also forced politically or otherwise unpopular professors to resign. The FEUE, however, has never played a role in the formation of a new government.

FEDERACION NACIONAL DE CHOFERES DEL ECUADOR (FNCE). National Federation of Chauffeurs of Ecuador. [Bus, Taxi and Truck Drivers.]

FEDERACION NACIONAL VELASQUISTA (FNV). A party originally founded in 1952 to support the candidacy of José María Velasco Ibarra, who had depended on an unorganized following in the past. The party was officially recognized by the Supreme Electoral Tribunal in 1968. It joined forces with other parties and ad-hoc movements to form the Movimiento Frente Popular Velasquista (MFPV) in supporting the presidential candidacy of Velasco Ibarra in the 1968 election. The MFPV candidate was victorious. In addition, the FNV elected 20 deputies and nine senators in the 1968 congressional election.

FERIAR. To sell cheaply, especially in an open market.

FERNANDEZ, JORGE. Born, January 16, 1912, Quito. Education: Central University of Quito, 1932-36. Literary man, public official; editor in chief of Ultimas Noticias, 1940-42; editor, El Comercio, 1942-44. Ecuadorean ambassador to the OAS, 1968-72. Author of several short-stories, and these novels: Antonio ha sido un hipérbole, 1933; Agua, 1937; Los que viven por sus manos, 1951.

FERNANDEZ DE HEREDIA, JUAN ANTONIO. Died, Saña, 1661. Public official. District attorney of Santiago, Chile, 1635; magistrate of same, 1645; Magistrate of Lima, 1653; appointed president of the Audiencia of Quito, 1661. He took possession January 23, 1662, when he reached Guayaquil, and died while journeying to the capital.

FERNANDEZ DE OVIEDO Y VALDEZ, GONZALO. Born, August, 1478, Madrid. Died, June 26, 1557, Valladolid(?). Historian. His Historia natural y general de las indias contains the accounts of the discovery of the Amazon and the founding of the city of Quito, but embraces many more historical events as well, not only in South America, but in Mexico.

FERNANDEZ DE RECALDE, JUAN. Born, Bilbao (Ciudad Rodrígo). Died, Quito, 1615. Educated at the University of Salamanca. Professor, public official. Alcalde del Crimen of Lima, 1586; magistrate of Lima, 1595; rector of the University of San Marcos, 1596-97; administrative investigator of Cuzco, 1600; governor of the Audiencia of Quito, 1609-12.

FERNANDEZ SALVADOR, JOSE. Born, January 23, 1775, Quito. Died, October 1, 1853, Quito. J. D. L. (civil and canon law), University of St. Thomas, Quito. Lawyer, public official, he served as states attorney, member of the city council (cabildo), mayor (alcalde) in Quito, and likewise in Riobamba, and as attorney and judge in the office of the Real Audiencia in the last years of the Spanish regime. He then became a senator in the Congreso of Gran Colombia. When Ecuador revolted to become an independent nation on its own, he drew up the new civil code based on the Code Napoleón, in 1831, but it was not effective until 1861 at Riobamba. Vice-president, 1830, interim president November 30, 1830. President of the Constituent Assembly at Riobamba, 1830. Afterward senator, minister of the Interior and Foreign Relations, Supreme Court judge.

FEUE see FEDERACION DE ESTUDIANTES ...

FIAMBRERA. Lunch box.

FID see FRENTE DE LA IZQUIERDA DEMOCRATICA

FIERRO, HUMBERTO. Born 1890, Quito; died, 1931. Modernist poet, chiefly influenced by the French symbolists, and the Peruvian, José María Eguren.

FIGON. Restaurant, eating house.

FLORES, JUAN JOSE. Born, July 19, 1800, Puerto Cabello, Venezuela. Died, October 1, 1864, on board the Sinyrk. No formal education. Military career. Governor of Pasto Province, 1823; general, 1829; chief of staff of the armed forces, 1835; president of

the Senate, 1837.   Presidency: (1) non-elected, age
30, 1830, interim president; (2) elected (Constituent
Convention), age 30, 1830, one term which was inter-
rupted in 1835 by various individuals who enjoyed
regional control; (3) elected (Constituent Convention),
age 39, 1839, one term which ended constitutionally,
1843; (4) non-elected, age 43, 1843, interim president until Constituent Convention was called together,
1843; (5) elected (Constituent Convention), age 43,
1843; one term, overthrown in 1845 by his former
political and military associate, Vicente Rocafuerte.

FLORES JIJON, ANTONIO.   Born, October 23, 1833, Quito.
Died, August 30, 1915, Geneva, Switzerland.   Education: J. D. , Central University of Quito, 1855.   Lawyer, politician, diplomat, writer.   Served at diplomatic posts in Colombia, France, England, the Vatican, Peru, and Spain.   He was in Europe when
elected to the presidency: popular vote, age 55, 1888,
one term, July 1, 1888 to August 31, 1892, ended
constitutionally.   Pedro José Cevallos, his vice-president, acted until Flores Jijón could return at the beginning of his term.

FLORES TORRES, MANUEL ELICIO.   Born, 1895, Riobamba.   Died, July 30, 1962, Quito.   Education:
J. D. , Central University of Quito.   Lawyer, teacher,
politician.   University professor, president of the
Supreme Court, many times deputy to nation's congress;
unsuccessful presidential candidate in 1948; important
spokesman of Ecuador's Conservative Party.

FLOTA MERCANTE GRAN COLOMBIANA.   Shipping firm
formed by Colombian and Ecuadorean businessmen,
June 8, 1946.   Beginning with a fleet of eight motor
ships of 5000 tons capacity each, it now has 27 vessels
of its own, and operates under lease or other arrangements 18 more.   The owned vessels have a total carrying capacity of 250, 000 tons and a cubic foot capacity
of 10. 64 million, of which 1. 88 million cubic feet are
refrigerated for carrying bananas, meats, fish, etc.
Regular service is maintained on 14 lines, to 147
ports in 32 countries.

FNCE   see   FEDERACION NACIONAL DE CHOFERES ...

FNV   see   FEDERACION NACIONAL VELASQUISTA

FOJEAR.   To read rapidly, to scan.

"FOUR DAYS' WAR. "   La Batalla (Guerra) de los Cuatro
    Días was the phrase used to describe the hostilities
    which broke out on August 29, after Neptalí Bonifaz
    Ascásubi, who had won the elections held in October
    1931, had been disqualified by the National Congress.
    A truce and cessation of fighting between opposing
    factions in the Army was only achieved on September
    1, after some 200. soldiers and civilians were killed
    and many more wounded.   See also BONIFAZ.

FREILE LARREA, CARLOS.   Born, July 15, 1892, Quito.
    Education: City and Guilds of London Institute, degree
    in civil engineering.   Civil engineer, gentleman
    farmer, politician.   President of the Guayaquil and
    Quito Railway Company; president of the Chamber of
    Agriculture (Zone 1); minister of Public Works, 1939;
    minister plenipotentiary to Great Britain.   Presidency:
    non-elected, age 40, took over August 28, 1932, after
    the resignation of Alfredo Baquerizo Moreno; was in
    turn overthrown and replaced by Alberto Guerrero
    Martínez after having occupied the presidency for five
    days.

FREILE ZALDUMBIDE, CARLOS.   Born, 1851, Quito.
    Died, August 21, 1926, Paris.   Gentleman farmer,
    politician.   Minister of Public Instruction, 1896;
    deputy from Pichincha Province and president of the
    Constituent Convention, 1906; president of the Senate,
    1911.   Presidency: non-elected, twice: (1) succeeded
    Eloy Alfaro when the latter was forced out of office
    in 1911; (2) succeeded Emilio Estrade after the latter's
    death in 1911, and was himself overthrown in 1912.
    In both cases he was president of the Senate--i. e. ,
    first in line of succession because the 1906 constitu-
    tion did not provide for a vice-president.

FRENTE DE LA IZQUIERDA DEMOCRATICA (FID).   A
    liberal center-left coalition which supported the candi-
    dacies of Andrés F. Córdova Nieto (president) and
    Jorge Zavala Baquerizo (vice-president) in the 1968
    presidential election.   The coalition was supported by
    three major parties: the PLR, PSE and CFP.   Its
    presidential candidate ran a close second while its
    vice-presidential candidate was victorious.

FRENTE DEMOCRATICO NACIONAL (FDN). An ad-hoc
coalition movement formed around the Radical Liberal
Party at national elections and composed of most
center-left political groups. The FDN supported the
presidential candidacies of Raúl Clemente Huerta (1956)
and Galo Plaza Lasso (1960). Both times the FDN
failed to elect its candidate and in 1956 it also failed
to prevent the conservative, Camilo Ponce Enríquez,
from gaining the presidency. The movement has two
objectives: to elect its candidate to the presidency
and to prevent a conservative takeover of the nation.
The present successor to the FDN is the FID.

FRENTE DE RESTAURACION NACIONAL (FRN). Ad-hoc
movement founded on May 4, 1971, with the objective
of returning Ecuador to constitutional normalcy
following José María Ibarra's assumption of dictatorial powers on June 20, 1970. The FRN was formed
by the Conservative Party, the Radical Liberal Party,
the Institutionalist Democratic Coalition, the Christian
Democratic Party, and the Democratic Union of
Rightist Workers.

FRENTE REVOLUCIONARIO DE ORGANIZACIONES POPU-
LARES (FROP). Organized in March, 1968 by Manuel
Araujo Hidalgo, for participation in the Presidential
election. It did not back any candidates, nor elect
any, but seems principally to have been a bargaining
tool in political give and take.

FRESCO. A cold drink made of sugar and fruit juice or
wine.

FRITZ, FRAY SAMUEL. Born, 1650, in Bohemia. Died,
1730, Lima. Missionary priest, early geographer,
engraver. Assigned to a mission to the Omaguas on
the Marañón River in 1687, Fritz soon became ill
and journeyed the length of the Amazon to Belém de
Pará, where he was able to obtain a cure for his
illness, but was imprisoned by the Portuguese authorities. Upon order of the King of Portugal he was released and escorted back to his missions. Afterwards he became aware of Portuguese occupation of
areas belonging to the Spanish crown on the upper
Amazon, journeyed to Lima, where he died upon
hearing that his efforts were of no avail. He is
credited with the first engravings of the city of Quito,

and maps of the entire course of the Amazon, 1705 onward.

FRN   see   FRENTE DE RESTAURACION NACIONAL

FROP   see   FRENTE REVOLUCIONARIO ...

FUROIANI   see   VILLAGOMEZ DE FUROIANI

- G -

GALAPAGOS ISLANDS (Officially Archipiélago de Colón). A group of 13 large, and many small islands located about 650 miles off the Ecuadorean coast. The island's land area is 3075 square miles. Isabella, the largest, contains about one half of the total area. Only four of the islands are inhabited. The Galápagos Islands were discovered by the Spaniard, Tomás de Berlanga, in 1535, and have formed part of Ecuador's National territory since February 12, 1832. The capital is San Cristóbal. Population (1968 est.), 3200. They form a national territory directly administered from Quito.

GALDIANO, JOSE MARIA   see   MOSQUERA-GALDIANO AGREEMENT

GALECIO, GALO. Born, 1908, Vinces, Los Ríos Province. Contemporary Ecuadorean painter.

GALLEGOS ANDA, ELIAS. Born, April 21, 1905, Ambato. Education: Central University of Quito, M. D. Physician, surgeon, politician; unsuccessful presidential candidate of the Communist-oriented Union Democratica Popular (UDP) in the 1968 election.

GALLEGOS LARA, JOAQUIN. Novelist. One of the "Grupo de Guayaquil" (q. v.).

GALLEGOS ORTIZ, EMILIO. Born, Guayaquil. Educated in Guayaquil and Spain. Historian, numismatist, philatelist, man of letters. Authority on Spanish colonial coinage, genealogy, and 19th-century commerce through Guayaquil. Member of numerous learned and cultural groups.

GALLEGOS TOLEDO, CAMILO. Born, September 19, 1895,

Latacunga. Education: Central University of Quito,
law.   Justice of the Superior Court in Quito and chief
justice of the Supreme Court; deputy to the National
Congress.   As head of the Supreme Court, he occupied
the presidency for one day (November 8, 1960), when
President José María Velasco Ibarra was overthrown
and vice-president Carlos Julio Arosemena Monroy
was in jail.

GARAYCOA, FRANCISCO JAVIER DE.   Born, Guayaquil,
January 3, 1772.   Died, Quito, December 3, 1859.
Doctor of theology, University of St. Thomas, Quito,
1798.   Clergyman.   Bishop of Guayaquil, 1838; second
archbishop of Quito, 1851-59.

GARCIA, BALTASAR.   Born, Guayaquil.   Died, 1883,
Guayaquil.   Early involved in patriot uprisings in
Guayaquil, fought against the Spaniards until the de-
cisive battle at Ayacucho, December 8, 1824, which
ended Spanish domination.

GARCIA, LIZARDO.   Born, April 26, 1842, Guayaquil.
Died, May 28, 1927, Guayaquil.   Education: secondary
schooling.   Banker, merchant.   Member and co-
founder of the Chamber of Commerce in Guayaquil,
1889-1905; minister of the Treasury, 1895; senator
from Guayas Province, 1898-1904; vice-president of
the Senate, 1898; manager of the Bank of Commerce
and Agriculture in Guayaquil, 1903.   Presidency:
popularly elected, age 63, 1905, one term, overthrown by Eloy Alfaro, in 1906.

GARCIA DE LEON Y PIZARRO, JOSE.   President of the
Audiencia of Quito, 1778-84.

GARCIA DE VALVERDE, N.   Born, Cáceres.   Public offi-
cial.   Magistrate of Quito and Lima; president of the
Audiencia of Quito, August 8, 1575; president of the
Audiencia of Guatemala, 1578-89.

GARCIA GOYENA, RAFAEL.   Born, Guayaquil, July 31,
1766.   Died, November 6, 1823, Guatemala.   Son of
a Spanish functionary who moved his family to Central
America when his son was ten years old, and of a
creole mother, native also of Guayaquil, he spent
three years in prison in Cuba (1784-1787) because of
a love affair and clandestine marriage.   He returned

to Guatemala, completed studies in law and remained there until his death. Identified with the Independence movement. Poet, author of a collection of poeticized "fables," and a number of other poetic works.

GARCIA HERRERA TREATY. May 2, 1890. A treaty between Ecuador and Peru in which both countries attempted to reach an equitable settlement of their boundary differences by modifying their extreme claims and recognizing their respective rights in the Amazon Basin. Under the arrangements made by the two plenipotentiaries, Peru was to receive Túmbez, Jaén and the ports of Maynas where she held establishments. To Ecuador were awarded the zones of the Maynas General Command which lay close to her, Macas, Quijos, and also the northern strip next to Colombia's frontier which usually goes by the name of Sucumbios Missions and which encloses Canelos. The treaty was not ratified by the two countries.

GARCIA MORENO, GABRIEL. Born, December 24, 1821, Guayaquil. Died, August 6, 1875, Quito. Education: J. D., Central University of Quito, 1844. Studied the physical sciences, mathematics, and theology in Paris. Lawyer, poet, politician. Senator from Guayas Province, 1853; rector, Central University of Quito, 1857; senator from Pichincha and Tungurahua Province, 1857; member of Governing Junta, May 1, 1859 to January 17, 1860; civil and military chief of Imbabura Province, 1868; minister of the Treasury, 1869. Presidency: (1) non-elected, age 39, 1861; convoked Constituent Convention; (2) elected (Constituent Convention), age 40, 1861, one term, which ended constitutionally, 1865; (3) non-elected, age 48, 1869, took over after overthrow of President Javier Espinoza; (4) elected (Constituent Convention), age 48, 1869, one term, assassinated in 1875.

GIL GILBERT, ENRIQUE. Born, July 8, 1912, Guayaquil. Novelist and member of the "Grupo de Guayaquil." Most important works: Los que se van: cuento del cholo y del montuvio (co-author), 1930; Yunga, 1933; Relatos de Emmanuel, 1939; and Nuestro pan, 1942.

GILBERT PONTON, ABEL A. Born, in 1890, Guayaquil. Died, May 26, 1965, Guayaquil. Education: University of Guayaquil, M. D. Physician, gentleman farmer, politician. Vice-rector of the University of Guayaquil; senator from Guayas Province; functional senator for agriculture from the Costa; vice-president of the Republic, 1842-52.

GIRON, TREATY OF. February 28, 1829. Signed by the delegates of Peru and Gran Colombia in which both parties recognized as their territorial limits the pre-independence boundary line. The Treaty was ratified on March 1, by Marshals de Lamar and Sucre, but proved to be only of preliminary importance, as Peru did not abide by its provisions, which fixed the southern frontier of Ecuador westward from the Amazon along the Río Yavarí to the sixth parallel of south latitude, to the Chinchipe, southwesterly to approximately the 79th degree of longitude and northwesterly along the Huancabamba watershed, the Río Chira, the Río Túmbez, to the Pacific.

GNP   see   GROSS NATIONAL PRODUCT

GOBERNADOR. An Indian official in the highland area appointed by the parish priest to act as a coordinator in ecclesiastical matters. In return for gifts from his fellow Indians, the gobernador initiates action on request for marriage ceremonies, funeral rites, and other ecclesiastical services. Gobernadores are appointed on a yearly basis.

GOBIERNO NACIONAL MILITAR REVOLUCIONARIO. Nationalist Military Revolutionary Government. The title given to the military junta established on February 15, 1972, presided over by General Guillermo Rodríguez Lara, who was almost at once made president of the nation. The official description of the government, however, remains as above.

GODIN, LUIS. Born, February 28, 1704, Paris. Died, September 11, 1760, Cádiz, Spain. Leader of the expedition sent by Louis XV of France to the Viceroyalty of Peru in cooperation with the King of Spain in 1735. The purpose was to carry out certain scientific observations and experiments along the equator, including the measurement of one degree of the arc of Earth's circumference.

GOMEZ DE BRACHO URDANETA, LUCIA. Born, 1940,

Guayaquil.   Educated in Guayaquil and Spain, as a
schoolteacher, librarian, archivist.   Poet of wide
recognition, with many awards both within Ecuador
and abroad.   Author of three published volumes of
poetry, Vuelo, Legia de amor, and Transparencia.
Married to Colonel Pedro Bracho U., one son.

GONZALEZ SUAREZ, FEDERICO.   Born, April 12, 1844,
Quito.   Died, December 1, 1917, Quito.   Jesuit clergyman.   Probably the best known and most renowned
clergyman of the Ecuadorean Church, he wrote extensively in the fields of history, politics, and theology.
He was archbishop of Quito from 1906-1917.   His full
name was Manuel María Federico del Santísimo Sac-
ramento.   His father was of Colombian nationality;
his mother, Ecuadorean.

GONZALEZ Y CALISTO, PEDRO RAFAEL.   Born, Quito,
October 24, 1939.   Died, Quito, March 27, 1906.
Doctor of theology, Pontifical Gregorian University,
Rome, 1866.   Clergyman.   Bishop of Ibarra, 1878;
deputy to the Congress of 1871 and 1878; senator from
Pichincha Province in the Congress of 1885 and 1886;
seventh archbishop of Quito, 1893-1906.

GORIBAR, NICOLAS JAVIER DE.   Born 1665, Quito; died
1736, Quito.   One of the most prominent 17th-century
Ecuadorean painters.   A student of Miguel Santiago,
probably his most famous works are the canvases
depicting the Old Testament prophets.   These can be
seen in the Compañía de Jesús, a church in Quito.

GOVERNMENT (LOCAL).   For administrative purposes
Ecuador is divided (as of June 1968) into 19 provinces
and the Galápagos Islands, 103 cantons, and 846
parishes (181 of which are urban and 665, rural).   In
each province there is a governor (gobernador); in
each canton, a political chief (jefe político); and in
each parish, a political lieutenant (teniente político),
all appointed by the president.   In the provinces there
is also a popularly elected provincial council (concejo
provincial) headed by a provincial prefect (prefecto
provincial).   Each canton constitutes a municipality.
Municipal government is in the hands of a popularly
elected municipal council (concejo municipal).   In the
provincial capitals the councils are headed by a
mayor (alcalde).   Urban parishes form part of a

municipality. Rural parishes, the lowest administrative subdivisions, are run by popularly elected parish
boards (junta parroquial) which elect a president from
their midst.

GOVERNMENT (NATIONAL). Ecuador has a republican,
presidential and representative form of government.
It is unitary with a division of power between the
executive, legislative, and judicial branches. Executive power is vested in the president of the Republic
who is elected by direct popular vote for a four-year
term and must stay out one term before being eligible
for reelection. The constitution also calls for a popularly elected vice-president who succeeds to the presidency during the chief executive's temporary or
permanent absence. Legislative power is exercised
by a bicameral National Congress--the Senate and the
Chamber of Deputies. The Senate is composed of 54
members, 39 directly elected (two from each province
and one from the Galápagos Islands) and 15 functional
senators. The Chamber of Deputies has 80 members
who are directly elected to represent the provinces in
proportion to their population. The constitution guarantees each province a minimum of two deputies (one
per 80,000 persons) and the Galápagos Islands, one
Senators are elected for a four-year term and deputies
for two years. Both can be re-elected indefinitely.
The judicial branch is composed of a supreme court,
superior courts, and other tribunals. Supreme court
justices are elected by Congress for a six-year term
and may be re-elected indefinitely. The number of
Supreme Court justices is not fixed but there have
been eight in the past. The Supreme Court appoints
justices to the Superior Courts. Justices may be
impeached only for negligence or a grave offense, as
determined by Congress.

GRAN COLOMBIA, 1821-1829. After independence, the name
given to the former Viceroyalty of Nueva Granada. It
included the present nations of Colombia, Venezuela,
Panama, and Ecuador. The usage is still current in
the name of the merchant fleet, Flota Grancolombiana,
and in a few similar expressions.

GROS MICHEL. The banana variety most commonly grown
in Ecuador for export purposes. It is not immune to
the Panama disease and its yield is smaller in compari-

son to other varieties, i. e. Cavendish, Lacatan, and
Valery.

GROSS NATIONAL PRODUCT.   In 1972 per capita income
was about $300.   About one half of the labor force
is engaged in agricultural pursuits; the rest are diver-
sified.   The average net growth in the GNP has been
4. 3% and agriculture has averaged approximately the
same as other economic sectors.   Bananas, cacao,
coffee, and sugar are the principal sources of revenue,
with petroleum rapidly increasing its share.

GRUPO DE GUAYAQUIL.   A literary circle formed by a
group of Ecuadorean novelists in 1930.   This group
was composed of José de la Cuadra, Joaquín Gallegos
Lara, Enrique Gil Gilberto, Demetrio Aguilera Malta
and Alfredo Pareja Diezcanseco.   Its members were
young novelists from Guayaquil whose intention was
to incorporate the "real" national life into Ecuadorean
novels, i. e., to describe the environment, customs
and mores of the people of the Ecuadorean coast and
the social injustices to which they were subject.
Their intentions are best demonstrated in a book of
short stories entitled Los que se van: cuentos del
cholo y del montuvio (1930), a collaborative effort by
three of the group's members, Gallegos Lara, Gil
Gilbert, and Aguilera Malta.

GUABUG.   Village in Chimborazo province where early
Indian peasant revolts took place (1904), presently
site of a cement factory and center of onion growing
and marketing which has made it prosperous and a
development model.

GUAGUA RUMI.   Quechuan word for the grinding stone held
in the hands when grinding corn or other grains on a
metate or grinding stone.   It means simply, "small
stone. "

GUAL, PEDRO.   Born, January 31, 1783 or 1784, Caracas,
now Venezuela.   Died, May 6, 1682, Guayaquil.
Doctor of civil and canon law, diplomat.   In 1835 he
was commissioned by the Ecuadorean government to
go to Europe, where he succeeded in getting recognition from Spain and other countries.   After 1848 he
returned to Caracas where he served as provisional
president and president of the Council of State.

Subsequently he again took residence at Guayaquil,
where he died. He was buried at Bogotá.

GUANGALA.   An archeological zone encountered primarily
    on the coast of Manabí Province, approximately in the
    latitude of La Plata Island, and the modern village of
    Chanduy.   Guangala zone sites date back to 100 B. C.

GUARANDA.   Capital of the province of Bolívar.   Population
    (1968 est.), 15,000.   In 1895 it was the center of a
    short-lived regional government.

GUARUMO (HUARUMO).   Musical instrument made from
    the wood of the tree of the same name (Cecropia
    peltata).   It is a wind instrument, about six feet in
    length, into the side of which is fitted a mouthpiece
    made of reed.   The low register tones are chiefly
    used as a part of an accompaniment, and to imitate
    the sounds of the lowing of cattle in certain folk
    festivities.

GUAYAQUIL.   Capital of Guayas province and the largest
    city in Ecuador.   Located on the Guayas River, about
    25 miles inland from the Gulf of Guayaquil, the city
    is one of the most important seaports of the west
    coast of South America.   The town was founded in
    1531 and was originally known as Santiago de Guaya-
    quil.   Population (1971 est.), 835,812.

GUAYAQUIL, TREATY OF.   September 22, 1829.   The
    treaty was the result of Colombia's victory over Peru
    at the Battle of Tarqui.   Article V of the treaty pro-
    vided that "both parties acknowledge as the limits of
    their respective territories those belonging to the
    ancient Viceroyalties of New Granada and Peru prior
    to their independence with such variations as they
    deem it convenient to agree upon..." and Article VI,
    that a boundary commission shall fix said limits.
    The treaty was duly drawn up and ratified by both
    countries, but the boundary question is still not com-
    pletely settled.   Called also the Larrea-Gual Treaty,
    because it was drawn by José de Larrea Loredo on
    behalf of Peru and Pedro Gual on behalf of the Great
    Colombian Union (New Granada).

GUAYAS.   Indian chieftain.   Legend has it that he com-
    mitted suicide after futile resistance to the Spaniards

under Orellana, who founded the city of Guayaquil, which bears the name of the chieftain and of his wife, Quil. Commemorative sculptures of the pair are on the south end of the Malecón, Guayaquil.

GUAYAS. A Province in Ecuador located on the Gulf of Guayaquil and containing 7368 square miles. Guayas Province is an agricultural region producing primarily export crops: i.e., cocoa, tobacco and some bananas and coffee. It is also rich in tropical woods and minerals. Population (1968 est.), 1,256,100.

GUAYAS RIVER. Principal river in Ecuador west of the Andes. The Guayas River and its tributaries play an important role in inland transportation in the coastal provinces. The largest and most modern port facilities in Ecuador are located on the west bank of the river near Guayaquil.

GUAYASAMIN, OSWALDO. Born, July 6, 1919, Quito. One of the best known Ecuadorean painters of the 20th century; he has exhibited in Europe and in most countries of the Western Hemisphere with general acclaim.

GUERRERO, JOSE ENRIQUE. Born, March 28, 1909, Quito. Education: School of Fine Arts, Quito. Julian Academy, Paris. Contemporary painter.

GUERRERO MARTINEZ, ALBERTO. Born, 1878, Guayaquil. Died, May 21, 1941, Guayaquil. Education: J.D., University of Guayaquil. Lawyer, politician. Deputy from Los Ríos Province, 1914; senator; vice-president of the Senate, 1923-24. Presidency: non-elected, 1932; took over after the "Four Days' War" and prepared for elections in the same year.

GUERRERO T., JORGE I. Born, Riobamba, 1912. Educated in the Instituto Nacional Mejía. Poet, writer, journalist. He has written extensively, been an active cultural envoy of his country, directed the radio station of the Casa de la Cultura in Quito.

GUEVARA, DARIO C. Born, April 8, 1905, Pelileo. Biographer, historian, essayist, teacher, folklorist. A professor in the Central University at Quito, Guevara has been principally responsible for the teaching of scientific folklore to both native and foreign investigators. One of his principal interests is the sociological importance of folklore. He is director of the Folklore Section of the Asociación Ecuatoriana de Antropología.

- H -

HACENDADO. Standard Spanish for a large land owner (hacienda), but in Ecuador traditionally it meant complete freedom to govern and exploit the Indian populace. Also, "hacendista."

HARMAN, ARCHER. Born, Staunton, Virginia, 1860. Died, October 9, 1911, Sulphur Springs, Virginia. Son of a colonel in the Confederate Army who had lost everything in the Civil War, young Harman left home in his teens and became through sheer hard work and application a leading railroad builder. During Eloy Alfaro's presidency he took over the construction of the Guayaquil-Quito railroad after others had failed. He died three years after completion of the project when he was thrown from a horse. He raised $20 million to capitalize the Compañía del Ferrocarril del Sur, as it was called, and his 57,069 shares, sold to the Ecuadorean government in April 1925 by his heirs, brought S/-2,400,000 at the then current rate of exchange (i.e., about $1,200,000).

HASSAUREK, FRIEDRICH. Born, October 8, 1831, Vienna. Died, October 3, 1885, Paris. North American diplomat who was stationed in Ecuador between 1861-65. His book Four Years Among Spanish-American, 1868, shows a keen observation of Ecuadorean life.

HERRERA, PABLO. Born 1820, Pujulí; died February 19, 1896. Historian and folklorist.

HERRERA-GARCIA TREATY. May 2, 1890. Through its representative, Dr. Pablo Herrera, Ecuador recognized the claim of Peru to territories held as of the date shown, and makes further territorial cessions. Dr. Antonio García signed for Peru. The treaty was ratified June 18 by the Ecuadorean Congress, but Peru refused to ratify.

HIDALGO, JOSE TELMO. Born, May 27, 1925, Sangolquí.
Education: J.D., Central University of Quito. Lawyer,
university professor of law, Central University; functional senator of labor for the Sierra, 1963; founder of
the Socialist Revolutionary Party of Ecuador, 1961;
secretary of the Federación de Trabajadores de Pichincha, a CTE affiliate, 1969.

HIGHWAYS. The Panamerican highway runs between the
two ranges of the Andes from the Colombian border
at Tulcán to Macará on the southern border with Peru,
a distance of 685 miles. Other highways link Guayaquil
with the Panamerican at Ambato, Riobamba, and
Tambo, as well as at Quito via Quevedo and Santo
Domingo. Highways from Quito to Esmeraldas, Guayaquil to Salinas, Guayaquil to Manta, Loja to Machala,
Cuenca to Machala, and others are either completed
or close to completion, connecting most of the principal cities and towns in their network and providing
transport underpinning for development on a much more
rapid scale than in the past. Oilfield explorations and
development in the area east of the Andes have prompted
especially rapid growth of highways there.

HIJO. Form of address used by the hacendado and the cura
in speaking to the Indian. Although the word is standard
Spanish for "son," the implication in this usage is one
of a servile relationship going beyond that of father and
son.

HOLINSKI, ALEXANDRE. Born, 1816. French traveller
who wrote L'Equateur, Scénes de la Vie Sud-Ameri-
caine, 1861, an interesting travel account devoid of
prejudices. The book is especially important for its
treatment of the abolition of slavery in Ecuador.

HOZ, PEDRO SANCHO DE LA. Born, Spain, December 8,
1547. Secretary of Fernando Pizarro. Historian of
the Conquest. He was accused of a plot to seize the
government in Chile and decapitated. Wrote Relación
de la conquista del Peru.

HUACHI. Site on the plains near Ambato where important
battles of the war for independence took place:
1) November 22, 1820, lost by the insurgents, and
2) September 12, 1821, when Sucre lost to the Royalists, José de Antepara was among those killed, and
Mires captured.

HUACHICOLA (also, guachicola). (Quechua.) A type of
   cheap, but potent, ordinary brandy. By extension,
   persons who are fond of the beverage, or overindulge
   are called by the same name--for example, the per-
   sonage in Jorge Icaza's El chulla Romero y Flores:
   Don Guachicola.

HUAIRO (also, huairu, or guayru). (Quechua.) A gambling
   device and the game played with it, especially at wakes
   and funerals. The device itself is somewhat like the
   die of Roman Italy and, like it, is made of bone, with
   various dots and circles engraved thereon. The game
   is thus apparently quite comparable to the rolling of
   dice. Money lost to the players is used to buy drinks
   and food for the mourners.

HUANCAVILCA. An aboriginal Indian tribe which inhabited
   the Province of Guayas at the time of the Spanish conquest. They were culturally and linguistically closely
   related to the Manta Tribe.

HUASICAMA. (Quechua.) The person who acts as a sort
   of door-keeper at the principal entrance to a hacienda.
   He cares for the barnyard fowls and cuts wood as well.

HUASIPICHAI. (Quechua.) A party given by the prospec-
   tive owner of a house built in a minga (q.v.). All
   those who participated in the minga are invited to eat,
   drink and dance at the expense of the new houseowner.

HUASIPUNGO. (Quechua: Huasi, "house" and pungo [pungu],
   "door.") A piece of land assigned by the landlord to
   the Indian in partial payment for services rendered.
   The huasipungo system, a form of peonage, has been
   outlawed by the Agrarian Reform Law of June 1964.
   Also, the title of Jorge Icaza's famous novel.

HUASIPUNGUERO. (Quechua.) The occupant of a huasipungo, who has only usufruct of the land as opposed
   to the "free Indian" who owns his.

HUAYNA CAPAC. Born, ca. 1450, Tomebamba, near Cuenca.
   Died, November 1525, Cuzco. The next-to-last Inca.
   The son of the Inca Emperor Túpac-Yupanqui, who
   continued his father's conquest of present-day Ecuador.
   The conquest was achieved when he married Paccha,
   the daughter of the vanquished king of the Scyris in

1487.   Huayna-Cápac ruled from 1475-1525.   By his
will he divided the empire between his two sons,
Huáscar receiving the southern, and Atahualpa the
northern part.

HUERTA, RAUL CLEMENTE.   Born, February 25, 1915,
Guayaquil.   Education: University of Guayaquil, Law.
Lawyer, politician.   Director of the Chamber of
Commerce in Guayaquil; president of the Provincial
Electoral Tribunal (Guayas Province); minister of the
Treasury; first president of the "Alliance for Progress
Commission" in Ecuador; founding member of the
Ecuadorean University Student Federation (FEUE);
head of Ecuador's Radical-Liberal Party; unsuccess-
ful presidential candidate, 1956.

HUMBOLDT, BARON ALEXANDER VON.   Born, September
14, 1769, Berlin.   Died, May 6, 1859, Berlin.   Education: University of Frankfurt/Oder, Göttingen;
School of Mines, Freiburg, Saxony, 1787-90.   Naturalist, explorer, humanist.   Humboldt arrived in Quito
on January 6, 1802, and traveled through Ecuador in
that year as well as part of 1803.   He studied the
Andean flora, volcanoes, and archeological antiquities,
ascended Chimborazo in June 1802, establishing a
new altitude record for his time.   While in Quito he
was a house guest of the Marquis of Selva Alegre.

HUMITA.   Tamal made from green corn ground into meal
and cooked in a steam bath with pieces of pork as a
filler.   The green corn husk is also used as a wrapper
instead of the dried.   In Quechua, choglo tanda or
choclotanda.

HURTADO DE MENDOZA, ANDRES (Marqués de Cañete).
Born, 1490; died, 1560, Lima.   Viceroy during ex-
pansion and settlement of new areas in Ecuador, he
authorized the foundation of Cuenca.

- I -

IBARRA.   Capital of the province of Imbabura.   Population
(1968 est.), 35,000.   Founded September 28, 1606 by
Cristóbal de Troya on orders of the president of the
Audiencia of Quito, Miguel de Ibarra.

IBARRA, MIGUEL DE. Born, Guipúzcoa, Spain. Died,
    April 29, 1608, Quito. Public official. Magistrate of
    Sante Fé, president of the Audiencia of Quito, Febru-
    ary 8, 1600 until his death. The city of Ibarra, capital
    of Imbabura Province, is named after him.

ICAZA, JORGE. Born, July 10, 1906, Quito. Education:
    medicine, Central University of Quito, 1924; National
    Conservatory (dramatic arts), 1927. Latin American
    novelist. He became famous with his novel Huasipungo
    (1934) depicting the plight of the Sierra Indians. Huasi-
    pungo is one of the first Latin American works to trans-
    form the indigenous novel from humanistic and romantic
    focus to social concern and protest. Other works:
    Barro de la sierra, 1933; En las calles, 1935; Cholos,
    1937; Media vida deslumbrados, 1942; Huairapamushcas,
    1948, El chulla Romero y Flores, 1958; Seis relatos,
    1958; Atrapados, 1970. Icaza was for many years
    Director of the National Library and has occupied
    other government posts. Presently, he serves as
    Ambassador to the U. S. S. R. (1972).

ICAZA-PRITCHETT TREATY (or Contract). September,
    1857. The government of Francisco Robles attempted
    to liquidate its debt to Great Britain by selling unused
    territory in the Amazon region to British bondholders.
    This transaction met with resistance from Peru, as
    part of the territory in question was claimed by her.
    Great Britain withdrew from the transaction when she
    realized the controversial nature of the territory her
    nationals were to receive under the contract.

ICFTU. International Confederation of Free Trade Unions.
    See also CONFEDERACION ECUATORIANA DE OBRE-
    ROS CATOLICOS.

ID see IZQUIERDA DEMOCRATICA

IERAC see INSTITUTO ECUATORIANO DE REFORMA
    AGRARIA Y COLONIZACION

ILLESCAS (El Inca Illescas). Older brother of Atahualpa,
    who was born in Quito. After Atahualpa's death, his
    general, Rumiñahui, attempted to consolidate his
    power and killed Illescas along with the rest of the
    royal family that had remained in Quito.

ILLINGWORTH, JUAN. Born, May 10, 1786, Stockport, England. Died, August 4, 1853, Guayaquil. English-born naval officer, founder of the Guayaquil Naval Academy and naval commander of Ecuador. An associate of Lord Thomas Cochrane of the Chilean Navy, also British, Illingworth was put in charge of a vessel which had as its mission the harrassment of Spanish Pacific coast installations. After being ship-wrecked, he went to Guayaquil where he joined the struggle for independence.

ILLINGWORTH BAQUERIZO, JUAN ALFREDO. Born, August 25, 1922, Guayaquil. Education: University of Guayaquil, law. Lawyer, banker, politician. Deputy from Guayas; vice-president of the Chamber of Deputies; dean of the College of Jurisprudence and Social Sciences, University of Guayaquil.

IMBABURA. Province located in the northern highlands. Area 450 square miles. Population (1968 est.), 202, 300

INCA. Title of the rulers of the Quechua-speaking peoples of what is now Peru, Ecuador, and Bolivia. The term is now used to refer to the Indians and their culture in an indiscriminate fashion.

INDIOS LIBRES. Indians who own their own land, thus "free Indians."

INDIOS PROPIOS. Indians living in a kind of serfdom and bought and sold with the land, thus "owned Indians."

INECAFE see INSTITUTO NACIONAL DEL CAFE

INEDES see INSTITUTO ECUATORIANO DE PLANIFICA-CION ...

EL INGA. El Inga sequence has been divided into two phases: the pre-ceramic and the ceramic. The pre-ceramic phase dates back to 7080 B. C. and is pos-sibly an Ecuadorean representative of a southward extension of the paleo-Indian chipped-point tradition. The ceramic period dates back to about 3000 B. C., when pottery making was introduced to Ecuador.

EL INGA SITE. The type of the pre-ceramic phase of El

Inga sequence, located about 20 miles east of Quito.

INGAPIRCA. A fortress located in Cañar province which is
the northernmost physical sign of the Inca Empire.
Ingapirca was declared a national monument on October
25, 1966.

INIAP   see   INSTITUTO NACIONAL DE INVESTIGACION
AGROPECUARIA

INSTITUTO ECUATORIANO DE PLANTIFICACION PARA EL
DESARROLLO SOCIAL (INEDES).   Ecuadorean Institute
for Social Development Planning.

INSTITUTO ECUATORIANO DE REFORMA AGRICOLA (IERAC).
The Agricultural Reform Institute, established in 1964,
and responsible for the redistribution of land to former
huasipungeros and agricultural workers in the arrimaz-
go system, had settled 16, 000 families on 70, 000
hectares with no compensation to former landholders
by 1971.   Minimum holdings were increased from 2. 3
to 3. 5 hectares.   Other redistribution has affected
10, 000 families on 328, 000 hectares, an average of
about 17 hectares per family.   New plans include the
settlement of 80 families on a small cattle growing
pilot area along the new highway to the Oriente.

INSTITUTO INDIGENISTA.   The center for study and aid to
the indigenous population of Ecuador, founded by Pío
Jaramillo Alvarado.

INSTITUTO NACIONAL DE INVESTIGACION AGROPECUARIA
(INIAP).   National Institute for Agriculture and Livestock Research.

INSTITUTO NACIONAL DEL CAFE (INECAFE).   National
Coffee Institute.

INTIRRAIMI [Inti raymi].   The Quechuan name for the
festival celebrated at the time of the summer solstice,
and therefore, since the Conquest and Christianization,
at the beginning of St. John's Day celebration (June 24).

IRITINGO.   (Quechua.)   Skinny, thin, having little flesh on
one's bones.

ISHPOSO.   (Quechua.)   Said of one who cannot control
urination, especially young children.

IZQUIERDA DEMOCRATICA (ID). A splinter group which
broke away from the Radical-Liberal Party, organized
by Rodrigo Borja in February 1970. The movement is
liberal in orientation and hopes to appeal to the masses.
It proposes to develop an ideology which will offer a
dynamic solution to problems of underdevelopment without sacrificing political liberties.

- J -

JACOME MOSCOSO, RODRIGO. Born, June 1, 1900, Quito.
Education: J. D. , Central University of Quito. Lawyer, diplomat, newspaperman. Newspaperman, 1919-
36; teacher-professor, Central University of Quito,
1925-35; diplomatic and consular posts in Italy, Hungary,
Belgium, Switzerland, Spain, Czechoslovakia; ambassador to the U. N. , 1966. Author: Treatises on International Law and Citizenship.

JAGUAY. A popular song form, usually heard during
harvest, and keeping time with the stroke of the
scythe. Other forms of the song are called jaichima,
jauilima, etc. The word derives from the nonsense
syllables repeated in the chorus.

JAMA-COAQUE. An archeological zone located between
Cape San Francisco and the Bahía de Caráquez on the
coast in Manabí province. The zone dates back to
220 B. C. There is an abundance of pottery artifacts
which bear a striking similarity to artifacts from
Meso-America.

JAMBELI. An archeological zone located around the mouth
of the Guayas river and extending across the Peruvian
frontier. The sites are coeval with the Guangala
phase, displaying some possible trade relations with
the former.

JARAMILLO ALVARADO, PIO. Born, 1889, Loja. Died,
1922. Education: University of Loja. Historian,
sociologist. Governor of Loja, professor of sociology
at the Universities of Quito and Guayaquil; founder of
the Instituto Indigenista. Politically a liberal, he
fought successfully against the assumption of the presidency by Neftalí Bonifaz in 1932. Probably the most
important Ecuadorean sociologist to date, his work,
El indio ecuatoriano, is a classic.

JEREZ, FRANCISCO DE. Born 1497?, Sevilla; died 1563? Historian. Secretary of Francisco Pizarro, and witness of the conquest. Author of Verdadera relación de la conquista del Perú y Provincia del Cuzco, llamada la Nueva Castilla.

JIJON CAAMAÑO Y FLORES, JOSE MANUEL. Born, 1920, Quito. Education: Loyola University Los Angeles (U. S. A.). Industrialist, politician. Many times deputy from Pichincha Province. Successor to his father, Jacinto Jijón y Caamaño, as the most important standard bearer of the Conservative Party (PC).

JIJON Y CAAMAÑO, JACINTO. Born, December 11, 1890, Quito. Died, 1950, Quito. Education: Central University of Quito. Industrialist, politician, historian, archeologist. Many times head of the Conservative Party; senator from Pichincha Province; presidential candidate in 1940; mayor of Quito. Considered the most important leader of the Conservative Party in the 20th century. Author of various historical and archeological studies, and Sebastián de Benalcázar (biography), 1936.

JIPIJAPA. Town in Ecuador which has given its name to "Panama" hats, woven in various parts of the country from the young leaves of a palm-like plant (Carloduvica palmata). The best quality hats have usually come from Montecristi, but Cuenca has also been a great center of production.

JIVARO. An Indian tribe with origin going far back in prehistory. The Jívaros are one of the best known of the primitive South American tribes. They live in the southern portion of Ecuadorean Oriente and number around 10, 000. Warlike by nature they have resisted outside invasions and have displayed indifference to other cultures or ways of life. Presently, most of them are culturally integrated. To the North American, the Jívaro is associated with the practice of shrinking human heads, called tsantsas.

JOCHA. A kind of tax or socially obligatory contribution to the prioste for a fiesta.

JORA. Sprouted corn used as the chief ingredient in the preparation of chicha, or native "beer."

JOTO. In Ecuador, an altered spelling and pronunciation of the word "cutu" (q.v.). In other parts of Ecuador and Colombia it means a bundle or pack, of clothing, etc. In Mexico it is a tabu word for a male homosexual.

JPN see JUNTA PATRIOTICA NACIONAL

JRSC see JUVENTUD REVOLUCIONARIA ...

JUAN Y SANTACILLA, JORGE. Born, 1712, Orihuela, Spain. Died, July 21, 1774, Cádiz. Spanish member of La Condamine expedition (see Condamine). Ship's captain.

JUNTA NACIONAL DE PLANIFICACION Y COORDINACION ECONOMICA. National Economic Planning and Coordination Board. A semi-autonomous government agency charged with directing socio-economic changes.

JUNTA PATRIOTICA NACIONAL (JPN). An ad-hoc coalition of most major political parties, whose purpose was to oust the military junta (1963-66) and return to constitutional government. The JPN was formed in 1965 and dissolved after its purpose was achieved a year later.

JUVENTUD REVOLUCIONARIA SOCIAL-CRISTIANA (JRSC). A youth group organized in 1965 by the Social Christian Movement (MSC).

- K -

K. This is not a letter of the Spanish alphabet, but it is employed in some transcriptions of Quechua (Kichwa in some Ecuadorean usage), and in foreign words and proper names. Words included in this compilation are found under the letter "Q."

KEMMERER COMMISSION. A group of economic experts headed by Princeton University Professor Edwin K. Kemmerer. The Commission was invited by President Isidro Ayora (1926) to analyze and reorganize the country's monetary and banking systems.

KINGMAN RIOFRIO, EDUARDO. Born, February 13, 1913,

Loja. Ecuadorean artist whose paintings have been
widely exhibited with acceptance in Europe and the
Western Hemisphere.

KISHKA (also, quishca). Townsman who speaks the Quechua
language and acts as intermediary in legal and other
matters where monolinguals are involved. He is more
than an interpreter in his functions.

- L -

LABOR UNIONS. The organization of labor began in the
1920's in Ecuador, but to this day organized labor
constitutes a small percentage of the total labor force.
Estimates of membership vary widely ranging from 5
to 40 per cent of the total employment in all sectors
with the first figure being the more realistic. The
difficulty in pinpointing union membership is variously
explanable by lax requirements pertaining to payment
of membership dues, and existence of a large number
of "paper unions." At present there are three independent unions. The largest confederation is the Com-
munist-controlled CTE (Confederación de Trabajadores
Ecuatorianos), organized in 1944. Second in numerical
importance is CEOSL (Confederación Ecuatoriana de
Organizaciones de Sindicatos Libres), founded in 1962
and politically unattached. Third is the conservatively
oriented CEDOC (Confederación Ecuatoriana de Obreros
Católicos), the oldest, organized in 1938.

LAFTA see ASOCIACION LATINOAMERICANA DE LIBRE
COMERCIO

LAGO AGRIO. The first of the newly developed oilfield
areas of Ecuador, east of the Andes, in Napo Province.

LAICHU. Among the saraguros (q. v.), "an Indian who has
become white"--i. e. , one who because of his economic
well-being is able to occupy the same position as a
white, to the point of hiring whites for menial labor,
but without the social and cultural implications which
exist elsewhere, as in the case of the "cholo" in Peru,
for example.

LA LIBERTAD. Principal oil port and refinery site on the
Pacific coast near Salinas in connection with the

exploitation of the Ancón oilfield.

LAMAR Y CORTAZAR, JOSE BENIGNO DE. Born, July 12, 1776, Cuenca. Died, October 11, 1830, San José, Costa Rica. Soldier, politician. In the Napoleonic period in Spain he served effectively in the Rosellon campaign and the defense of Zaragoza. Sent to America he fought against San Martín in the insurgent attack on Callao, Peru. He soon joined the rebellion against Spain, however, and was a commander of the Peruvian troops at the Battle of Ayacucho, December 9, 1824, which broke Spanish power forever. Lamar was elected president of Peru on August 27, 1827, and soon led his people in a war against Gran Colombia. He previously had forced Sucre to resign as president of Bolivia. Sucre then led the Colombians successfully at the battle of Portete de Tarqui, on the outskirts of Cuenca, February 26, 1829. Two days later Lamar and Sucre signed the Treaty of Girón. On June 7, 1829 Lamar was deposed by his own officers, and went into exile in Costa Rica, where he died.

LARRAIN, SANTIAGO DE. Born, Villa Arana, Navarra. Clergyman, public official. President of the Audiencia of Quito, July 27, 1715 until May 17, 1717, the year in which the Audiencia was temporarily incorporated into the Viceroyalty of New Granada; Knight of the Order of St. James (Santiago).

LARREA ALBA, LUIS. Born, October 25, 1895, Guayaquil. Education: Military Academy in Quito and Santiago de Chile. Military career, politician. Military attaché in Italy and Peru; intendant general of the police in Guayas Province, 1925-29; deputy from El Oro Province to the 1928 Constituent Convention; minister of National Defense; founder of the Ecuadorean Socialist Revolutionary Vanguard (VSRE); functional senator for the Armed Forces, 1933. Presidency: non-elected, age 37, in 1931, when he took over after the overthrow of Isidro Ayora. He was forced out of office after attempting to institute a dictatorship that same year.

LARREA-GUAL TREATY. September 22, 1829. See GUAYAQUIL, TREATY OF.

LARREA Y LOREDO, JOSE DE. Born, March 19, 1790,
    Huaraz, Peru. Died, 1831, Lima. Educated for the
    law in the Lima Seminary of Santo Toribio. Politician
    and diplomat. Plenipotentiary to Gran Colombia for
    the boundary negotiations in 1829, and later minister
    of State for Peru.

LASCANO BAHAMONDE, ALEJO. Born, July 17, 1840,
    Jipijapa, Manabí. Died, December 3, 1904, Guayaquil.
    Education: J. D. Educator, lawyer. Served as first
    rector of the University of Guayaquil.

LATACUNGA. Capital of Cotopaxi Province. Population
    (1968 est.), 35,000.

LAVAYEN, FRANCISCO DE PAULA. Born, 1791, Guaya-
    quil. Died, 1860, Quito. Member of the original
    independence group at Guayaquil. Fought against the
    Spanish. Opposed Flores' presidency and was exiled,
    but joined forces of Rocafuerte. Occupied several
    important government posts after triumph of the latter.
    Never sought rank higher than colonel in the military.

LEGARDA, BERNARDO DE. Born early 1700's; died May
    31, 1773. The best Ecuadorean sculptor of the 18th
    century. His most important work is the "Virgin of
    Quito."

LEMOS RAYA, FAUSTINO. Colombian national who assas-
    sinated Gabriel García Moreno on August 6, 1875.

LEON, FRANCISCO JAVIER. Died, August 10, 1880. Edu-
    cation: J. D. Public service: lawyer, politician;
    minister of Interior, 1873; minister of Foreign Rela-
    tions; vice-president of the Republic, 1869. Presi-
    dency: non-elected, 1875, completed term of Gabriel
    García Moreno, who was assassinated.

LEON, JOSE VICENTE. Born, January 1773, Latacunga.
    Died, February 28, 1839, Cuzco, Peru. Left his
    entire estate for the establishment of a school at
    Latacunga, which bears his name.

LEON DONOSO, PEDRO. Born, January 18, 1895, Quito.
    Died, 1956, Quito. Educated at the National School of

Fine Arts, Quito. Professor in the National School of
Fine Arts from 1924. Cultivated all types of painting:
oil, decorative art, aquarelle, theater sets and cur-
tains, portraitist. Followed the advanced French
Schools, as for example the surrealists. Notable
paintings on colonial Quito.

LEON GIXON [JIJON], TOMAS. Born, Quito. Doctor of
theology and canon law, University of Santo Tomás.
Sent to Rome to promote the beautification of Mariana
de Jesús Paredes, his biography of the future saint
was published in Madrid in 1754.

LEORO FRANCO, GALO. Born, December 15, 1926,
Imbabura. Education: licentiate in social sciences
and J. D. , Central University, Quito. Diplomat. He
began his career in the Ecuadorean foreign service
as a vice consul in New York, 1953. Since then he has
served in Washington, Mexico, and in connection with
international conferences. Reached full rank as ambassador of career in 1968. Subsecretary general,
Foreign Relations, 1970-71; ambassador to the Dominican Republic, 1971-72; ambassador and permanent
representative of Ecuador to the Organization of
American States, 1972.

LETAMENDI, MIGUEL DE. Born, Venezuela. Sergeant
in the Spanish army who became an insurgent with
colonel's rank and fought in the 1820 uprising at
Guayaquil; later became an Ecuadorean citizen.

LEVI CASTILLO, VICENTE. Born, April 5, 1928, Guayaquil. Education: Colombia University, Dorothy Kane
School, New York. Politician, newspaper writer,
engineer, computer programmer, novelist. Founder
and leader of the Independent Republican Movement
(MRI), 1961, which was officially recognized as a
party in 1969 by the Supreme Electoral Tribunal and
is now known as the Independent Republican Party (of
Ecuador) (PRIE); elected deputy from Guayas, 1966,
1968; supporter of Velasco Ibarra.

LIBERACION POPULAR see MOVIMIENTO FRENTE ...

LIUT, ELIA. Italian aviator who established the Ecuadorean National Aviation Service and Air Force, 1920.

LIZARAZU, JUAN DE. Born in Navarre. Died, Quito
1645. Public official. Knight of the Order of St.
James (Santiago). President of the Audiencia of Quito,
1642-45.

LLACTA. Country, region, place where one was born.
Facetiously employed, it means the backwoods, sticks,
country.

LLAMBO. Quechuanism which means level, polished,
smooth.

LLERENA, JOSE ALFREDO. Born, July 2, 1912, Guayaquil. Ecuadorean journalist, novelist, and historian,
presently an editor of the Quito daily El Comercio.
Most important works: Agonía y paisaje del caballo
(poems); Segunda vida de una santa (short stories),
1953; Frustración política en 22 años (history), 1959.

LLONA, NUMA POMPILIO. Born, Guayaquil, 1832. Died,
Guayaquil, April 5, 1907. Poet of the romantic movement, his works reflect the usual characteristics of
the period. He has been likened to Edgar Allan Poe
in his ideas. He was crowned "poet of the nation" in
1904.

LOCRO [ROCRO]. A kind of soup made with especially
chosen small potatoes, probably a separate species,
with some achiote added for color, and perhaps flavored
also with coriander. Often served at the end of a
meal.

LOJA. Capital of the Province of Loja, situated near the
border with Peru. The city was founded by Alonso
de Mercadillo in 1546. Elevation 7000 feet. Population (1968 est.), 35,000.

LOJA. Southernmost province of highland Ecuador. Area,
4445 square miles. Population (1968 est.), 348,900.

LONGO. An adult Indian who has not reached the age of
18 or who has as yet not fulfilled any civic responsi-
bilities (i.e., serving as mayor, dancer, etc.).
Longo is more frequently used in derogatory fashion
by the inhabitants of the coast in describing the highland people. In such a case the term becomes
synonymous with "mono" or monkey, when Sierra

inhabitants refer to those of the Costa.   Also it is in
popular usage as a term of endearment used of men
by women as an equivalent of the English "boy friend."

LOPEZ, MODESTO.   Born, Ibarra, Imbabura Province.
Died, 1900? Quito.   Civil Engineer.   Prior to the time
of García Moreno in the presidency, there were no
professional engineers in Ecuador.   López was the
first and was surveyor and civil engineer for the construction on most all of the basic railroad routes in
the Andean zone, the first being from Quito to Sibambe.

LOPEZ DE DICASTILLO, FRANCISCO.   Born, Vizcaya,
1625.   Died, Puebla, 1706.   Licenciado en leyes,
University of Alcalá de Henares.   Lawyer, public
official.   Magistrate in Bogotá, 1684; magistrate in
Santo Domingo, 1681; district attorney, Lima, 1689;
magistrate in Lima, 1691; president of the Audiencia
of Quito, 1703-5; member of the Council of the Indies,
died on his way to assume his post.   Knight of the
Order of Calatrava.

LOS RIOS.   Province in Central Ecuador located on the
Western slopes of the Andes.   Area 3076 square miles.
Population (1968 est.), 319, 100.

LP   see   MOVIMIENTO FRENTE POPULAR VELASQUISTA

LUNA YEPEZ, JORGE.   Born, December 21, 1909, Quito.
Education: J. D. , Central University of Quito, 1940.
Lawyer, politician-historian.   Deputy from Pichincha
Province to National Congress, 1934, 1942, 1952-58;
co-founder of the Ecuadorean Nationalist Revolutionary
Action, a right-wing party, 1941; author: Explicación
del ideario de ARNE, 1950; Síntesis histórica y geo-
gráfica del Ecuador, 1951.

                           - M -

MACANA.   A kind of shawl (rebozo), usually with a long
and intricately woven fringe.

MACAS.   Capital of the province of Morona-Santiago.   Population (1968 est.), less than 10, 000.

MACHALA.   Capital of the province of El Oro.   Population
(1968 est.), 50, 000.

MACHALILLA. An archeological phase named after a site on the coast of Southern Manabí Province. The Machalilla phase dates back to 1370 B. C. Figurines are rare but pottery is the earliest in Ecuador to make use of painting.

MACHANGARA. A small river that runs through Quito.

MACHO. As noun: male individual who seeks always to demonstrate his masculinity in his social relationships and daily living.

MAINAS. The area included on both sides of the Marañón River (i. e., the river basin), known in the late colonial period as "Maynas y Quijos." Largely unsettled and effectively occupied only by missionary establishments. The Royal Decree of 1802 (q. v.) separated them from the control of the bishop of Quito and placed them under the archbishop of Lima. Mainas is nowadays the name applied by Peru to the area awarded her under the protocol of Rio de Janeiro in 1942, but the arrangement is still not accepted as final by Ecuador.

MALABA. An Indian tribe which most likely descended from the Puruhá tribe of the Sierra. The Malaba lived in Esmeraldas Province in the 17th century, but fled from the advancing Spaniards to the Mataje River Valley in northernmost Ecuador. There exists no knowledge of their whereabouts today.

MALACATO see PALTA

MALDONADO Y SOTOMAYOR, PEDRO VICENTE. Born, 1709, Riobamba. Died, November 17, 1748, London. Education: "San Luis Seminary," Quito, exact sciences. Ecuadorean geographer whose major contribution was the improvement of the "Map of the Kingdom of Quito." He was named governor and captain general of Atacames and Esmeraldas, 1738. Chamberlain to his Majesty Philip V, he was member of several prestigious scientific societies in France and Spain. Worked with the Condamine expedition (q. v.).

MALO VALDIVIOSO, BENIGNO. Born, 1805, Cuenca. Died, April 2, 1870, Cuenca. Education: J. D., University of Azuay, Cuenca. Statesman, diplomat,

educator, writer. First Rector, University of Azuay
(January 1, 1868). His works were published under
the title Escritos y discursos, Quito, 1940. Founder
of an important preparatory School in Cuenca, now
named for him.

MALTA. Large earthenware jar used to keep liquids.

MANABI. Coastal province located in north central Ecuador. Area 7602 square miles. Population (1968 est.),
751, 500.

MANAVALE. Useless, inept.

MANCHENO CAJAS, CARLOS. Born, 1902, Riobamba.
Education: military education. Soldier who achieved
the rank of colonel; Minister of National Defense,
1947. Presidency: non-elected, age 45, 1947, when
he overthrew José María Velasco Ibarra, but resigned
after a few days due to lack of support by the armed
forces.

MANOSALVAS, JUAN. Born, June 24, 1840, Quito. Died,
February 23, 1906, Quito. Artist, teacher of painting.
Studied under Alessandro Marini and Mariano Fortuny
in Rome.

MANTA. Trading people, which at the time of the Spanish
conquest inhabited most of Ecuador's coast. They
also were referred to as the League of the Traders
or "those with tattooed faces."

MANTA. Seaport in Manabí Province. Since it is the point
of convergence of a number of roads and highways inland, it is important in exports in the region not served
by Guayaquil. It has an airport. The Technological
and Agricultural Institute of Manabí is located there.

MANTEÑO. Major archeological zone extending along the
coast from Bahía de Caráquez to the Island of Puná,
and inland over the Cerro de Hojas and southern
Manabí Province. The zone, which dates back to A. D.
850, is rich in pottery and figurines. The phase is
named after the Manta tribe which occupied this
region.

MAPA. Used either as a noun or an adjective, it means

filth, dirt, garbage; dirty, stupid, obscene.

MAPASINGUE, TREATY OF. January 25, 1860. Climaxed
a war between Ecuador and Peru, which the latter
won. The treaty emphasized the validity of the Peruvian title to much of the Amazon region, and likewise
declares null and void the Ecuadorean adjudication of
lands to British bondholders (See ICAZA-PRITCHETT
TREATY). The treaty was ratified by President
Castillo of Peru and General Franco of Ecuador but
rejected by the Congresses of both nations.

MAPIOSO. Dirty, unbathed, afraid of soap and water.

MARAÑON, ESTEBAN. Licentiate in law. Judge of the
court in Lima, named dean of judges at Quito, and
judge-auditor (juez de residencias). Interim president
of the Audiencia of Quito from 1593 until 1599, when
he died.

MARAÑON RIVER see AMAZON

MARCOS, FRANCISCO. Ecuadorean delegate to the first
Postal Congress of the Americas and Spain in 1883.
The Congress established special postal rates for the
nations of the Western Hemisphere and Spain.

MARQUES DE SELVA ALEGRE see MONTUFAR Y
FRASSO ... and MONTUFAR Y LARREA ...

MARTINEZ DE LANDECHO, JUAN. Appointee to the presidency of the Audiencia of Quito, 1582?, but died in
Panamá on the way to take office.

MARTINEZ MERA, JUAN DE DIOS. Born, March 9, 1875,
Guayaquil. Died, October 27, 1955, Guayaquil.
Education: University of Guayaquil. Lawyer, politician; secretary of the Guayaquil Council; vice-rector
of the Colegio Vicente Rocafuerte; president of the
Chamber of Deputies; minister of the Treasury. Presidency: elected (popular), age 57, 1932, one term;
was impeached and turned out by Congress, 1933.

MATA, GONZALO HUMBERTO. Born, April 21, 1904,
Quito. Ecuadorean novelist who describes the plight
of the Sierra Indians. Most important works: Sumag
Allpa, 1940; Sanagüin, 1942.

MATA PONCE DE LEON, MATEO DE LA.   Born, Requeña.
Public official.   President of the Audiencia of Quito,
January 20, 1691 to 1701; named to membership in
the Council of the Indies, but did not accept.   He was
then appointed dean of the magistrates of the Audiencia
of Lima.

MAYORAL.   Straw-boss, group leader; principal servant
in the household.

MCDN   see   MOVIMIENTO CIVICO DEMOCRATICO NA-
CIONAL

MEJIA DEL VALLE Y LEQUERICA, JOSE JOAQUIN.   Born,
May 24, 1775, Quito.   Died, October 27, 1813 (yel-
low fever), Cádiz, Spain.   Education: Doctor of
Theology, 1806, Quito.   Professor, orator.   Probably
the most eloquent public speaker in Ecuadorean history,
he participated as substitute delegate of the Viceroyalty
of the New Granada to the Cortes of Cádiz (1818);
fought for the rights of Indians and Negroes in the New
World, and for equal representation of the Americas in
the Cortes of Cádiz.   His presence in Spain was due
to his previously having joined the botanical expedition
of José Celestino Mutis, studying the flora of South
America.   With him, or shortly thereafter, he returned
to Spain where he fought in the resistance against
Napeoleon's invading army.

MERA MARTINEZ, JUAN LEON.   Born, June 28, 1832,
Atocha (near Ambato).   Died, December 13, 1894,
Ambato.   Historian, poet, author of the text of the
National Anthem, 1865.   Considered one of the pre-
cursors of Ecuadorean folklore studies.

EL MERCURIO.   Cuenca daily newspaper with a circulation
of 5000.   It was founded on October 22, 1924, and
has a conservative editorial policy.   Its director is
Miguel Merchán Ochoa.

MEREJO.   Ecuadoreanism for tonto, "fool."

MERINO, PABLO.   Born, Guayaquil.   J.D., University of
St. Tomás, Quito.   Lawyer, politician, deputy from
Guayas to the Convention of Ocaña, 1828; counselor
of state, 1838; president of the Chamber of Deputies,
1845; vice-president of the republic during the Roca

administration; minister of the Interior, 1849; Ecuadorean representative of the First American Congress
in Lima.

MESA.   Polling place.   In the 1968 national election there
were a total of 3366 polling places distributed over
the nation to serve 1,198,987 registered voters.   Each
polling place serves a maximum of 400 registered
voters, the list of which is obtained from the civil
registry (Registro Civil).   Each polling place is at-
tended by five election officials who supervise the
election.

MFPV   see   MOVIMIENTO FRENTE POPULAR VELAS-
QUISTA

MIDEROS, VICTOR MANUEL.   Born, March 28, 1888,
Ibarra.   Died, 1962(?), Quito.   Bachiller, Seminario
Menor de San Diego, medicine; 1906-1913, Central
University of Quito.   Painter.   Professor, National
School of Fine Arts; Director, 1933 onward.   Member
of various academies in Ecuador and Europe.   Winner
of medals in various expositions, his works are in
many private collections and public buildings in
Ecuador.

MILAGRO.   An archeological site located in the region
occupied earlier by the Daule and Tejar phases (i.e.,
Guayas basin and the Province of El Oro).   The phase
dates back to A.D. 1300's and coincides well with
the distribution of settlements of the Huancavilca tribe.

MINGA.   An invitation extended by a person or organization
to a large number of people of a village to help finish
a job instead of paying to have it done by professionals.
This cooperative effort may involve the construction of
a house, road, public building, etc.   The minga, is
always voluntary, the benefactor paying his helpers in
food and drink.   "Voluntary" sometimes comes to sig-
nify obligatory, however, due to social pressure from
the organizer(s).   Often used in the plural mingas, in
the same sense.

MIRES, JOSE.   Born, Spain.   Died, 1824, Guayaquil.   Spanish
soldier who early became disgusted with the manner
in which the government of the colony was conducted
and joined dissident elements in the movement for the

independence of New Granada. He was captured on
July 4, 1811, after the Battle of San Esteban, and
taken in chains to Cádiz, thence to Ceuta, where he
managed to escape. Back in New Granada, he re-
joined the insurgents, participated in various skirmishes
including the Battle of Boyacá, and occupied Popayán.
Afterward, Mires was in Guayaquil, and commanded in
the Battle of Yaguachí, August 19, 1822, where the
insurgents were again victorious. He suffered defeat
at Guachi (Ambato), and was captured by Aymerich.
Freed, he fought at Pichincha, May 24, 1822. After
independence he was governor of Pasto (Colombia),
and later passed to Guayaquil, where he was assassinated before the separation of Ecuador from the
Great Colombian Union.

MISION ANDINA DEL ECUADOR. International socio-
economic development agency created by the International Labor Organization with the governments of
Peru, Bolivia, and Ecuador, 1951.

MITA. A colonial labor system whereby the Indians were
assigned to act as servants, miners, fishermen, etc.
to the population of European origin. The system
originated with the Incas, and was continued under
Spanish domination. Abolished in 1601, it was continued under a different name until the 20th century.
See CONCERTAJE.

MITAYO. An Indian assigned to work under the mita.

MITIMAES. Term used to describe or designate the groups
of Indians, which, for political reasons, were trans-
ferred from one region to another, beginning in Incan
(pre-Colombian) times.

MNA see MOVIMIENTO FRENTE ... and MOVIMIENTO
NACIONAL ...

MNR see MOVIMIENTO NACIONAL REVOLUCIONARIO

MODUS-VIVENDI AND CONVENCION ADICIONAL DE 1937.
Two agreements signed by the Vatican and President
Federico Páez leading to re-establishment of diplomatic relations between Ecuador and the Holy See,
abrogated since 1897. Provisions of these agreements included: 1) the church must respect the individual's right of liberty and conscience; 2) the church

must not interfere in politics or governmental affairs;
3) the church would be henceforth allowed to keep the
property it held and to acquire more; 4) the church
was allowed to have its educational institutions as long
as they met national standards; and 5) the Holy See
could elect the Ecuadorean hierarchy as long as their
choices were acceptable to the government.

MOGROVEJO, Toribio Alfonso (Santo). Born, 1538, May-
orga, León, Spain. Died, March 23, 1606, near
Lima. Missionary, and later, archbishop of Lima.
Founder of a seminary in Lima in 1591. In his early
missionary years he visited all of the foundations within his bishopric, and was principally responsible for
the application of the new rules of church conduct determined by the Councils of Trent (1545-1563) in Quito.
Beatified by Pope Innocence XI, June 26, 1679, he was
proclaimed a Saint by Benedict XIII, April 27, 1726.

MONCAYO Y ESPARSA, PEDRO. Born, July 29, 1807,
Ibarra. Died, 1888, Santiago de Chile. Education:
Doctor of Civil and Ecclesiastical Law, Central Uni-
versity of Quito. Lawyer, publicist. Deputy from
Guayas province, 1846; Commercial Attaché in France
and Chile. Published and wrote for the periodical
El Quiteño Libre (1833), in which he attacked the
government of Juan José Flores.

MONGE, CELIANO. Born, Ambato. Education: Colegio
San Gabriel in Ambato, specializing in philosophy,
rhetoric, and mathematics. Educator, journalist,
writer. Private secretary of Eloy Alfaro, deputy in
the National Congress in 1906. One of the great
literary geniuses of Ecuador whose major works
appeared in the four Ambato weeklies, El Combate
(1883-87); El Atomo (1888); La Alborado (1888); and
La Pluma (1890).

MONO. "Monkey." A word used in derogatory fashion
by the highland people against the people of the coast.

MONTALVO, ABELARDO. Born, June 1, 1876, Quito.
Died, December 26, 1950, Quito. Education: J.D.,
University of Quito. Lawyer, politician. Deputy and
senator from Pichincha province; deputy to the Con-
stituent Convention of 1906; professor of law at Central
University; rector of the Colegio Nacional Mejía.

Presidency: non-elected, age 57, 1933; replaced Juan
de Dios Martínez Mera when the latter was impeached
and turned out of office; stayed on until the popular
election of José María Velasco Ibarra in 1934.

MONTALVO FIALLOS, JUAN. Born, April 13, 1832,
Ambato. Died, January 7, 1889, Paris. Essayist
and writer. One of the best known Ecuadorean authors.
A liberal, he attacked the García Moreno regime from
exile in Colombia, and claimed that it was his pen that
killed García Moreno when the latter was assassinated
outside the Government Palace on August 6, 1875.

MONTECRISTI. City in Manabí province. Center of the
Panama hat industry. Population (1968 est.), 12,000.

MONTES, TORIBIO. Military officer, public official.
Spanish general who served as president of the Audiencia of Quito 1812-17, during which time he attempted
to suppress the growing movement for independence.

MONTUFAR, CARLOS DE. Born, November 1780, Quito.
Died, July 31, 1816 (firing squad), Buga (or Popayán),
Colombia. A military leader; son of Juan Pío Montúfar y Larrea. Education: secondary education in
Spain. He accompanied the Baron von Humboldt on
his expedition in America. Fought with the Spanish
forces against Napoleon, rising to the rank of lieutenant colonel. Upon his return to America he was
a participant in a great number of battles of the Independence movement in Gran Colombia, especially in
the Ecuadorean area, becoming a colonel at the time
of his capture and execution. He also organized one
of the several insurgent governing bodies in 1810.

MONTUFAR, PEDRO see following entries

MONTUFAR Y FRASSO, JUAN PIO [Marqués de Selva
Alegre]. Born, 1661, Granada, died, July 14, 1761,
Quito. Military leader. Twenty-third president of
the Real Audiencia of Quito, July 3, 1747. Entered
the office on September 21, 1753, and served to 1761;
commander of the order of St. James (1712). Quito,
Ambato and Latacunga suffered seriously from disastrous earthquakes during his term in office (1755
and 1757). He was father of the second marqués of
the same name.

MONTUFAR Y LARREA, JUAN PIO DE [Marqués de Selva
Alegre]. Born, June 20, 1759, Quito. Died, 1818,
in exile, Cádiz, Spain. Son of the Marqués de Selva
Alegre who governed the Presidency of Quito, 1753-
61. One of the leaders of the independence move-
ment. It was on his hacienda, in the Valley of Los
Chillos (near Quito), that the first meeting of the
independence leaders took place on December 25, 1808.
These were: José Luis Riofrío, Juan José Salinas
(Zenitagoya), Antonio Ante, Juan de Dios Morales,
José Manuel Rodríguez de Quiroga, Juan Pablo Arenas,
Francisco Javier de Ascázubi, and Pedro Montúfar.
On August 10, 1809 a junta of the patriots was formed
and Montúfar elected its president. This was the first
independent governmental body set up in the Spanish
colonies, but it was of course destroyed in 1810.
Montúfar renounced his title of nobility in 1815.

MONTUVIO. Name given to the peasantry of the Coastal
lowlands. The word montuvio carries the same connotation in the lowlands as does chagra in the highlands.

MON Y VALVERDE, JUAN ANTONIO. Public official.
President of the Audiencia of Quito, appointed April
29, 1790. Member of the Council of the Indies.

MORA BOWEN, ALFONSO. Born, July 7, 1909, Quito.
Education: Catholic University of Quito, University
of Michigan, J.D., University of Rome. One of
Ecuador's most prestigious lawyers and authors; attorney general, member of several cultural and legal
institutions.

MORALES, JUAN DE DIOS. Born, April 13, 1767, Rionegro,
Departament of Antioquía, Colombia. Died, August 2,
1810, Quito. Lawyer who defended Francisco Espejo,
precursor of Ecuadorean independence. Responsible
for formulating the plan by which the governing junta
was to be established to take over from the Spanish
authorities in the event of independence. Imprisoned
and killed in jail-break at Quito, 1810. Known as the
"Soul of Ecuadorean Independence."

MORA VEINTIMILLA, ALFONSO. Born, February 26, 1919,
Cuenca. Education: Central University of Quito, Law.
Lawyer, politician. Several times head of the Radical
Liberal Party.

MORENO PEÑAHERRERA, JULIO E. Born, October 20, 1880, Quito. Education: Law, Central University of Quito, no degree. Lawyer, sociologist, politician. Member of the 1929 Constituent Convention; minister of the Interior, 1826-30; president of the Senate, 1939. Presidency: non-elected, age 59, 1940. He took over from Andrés F. Córdova Nieto for less than a month until elections were held.

MORGA SANCHEZ, GARAY Y LOPEZ DE GARFIAS, ANTONIO DE. Born, November 29, 1559, Seville. Died, July 21, 1636, Quito. Education: Doctor of Civil and Canon Law, Salamanca. Public official. Governor of Manila; Alcalde de Crimen (Penal Court Judge), Mexico; President of the Audiencia of Quito, 1615-36. During his term Guayaquil was devastated in the repulse of an attack by the Dutch pirate, Jorge L'Hermetemas (1624).

MORLACA. Popular name applied to the chola of Cuenca, which is extended as an adjective with the conventional gender endings to apply to anything or anyone from Cuenca; Cuencan.

MORONA SANTIAGO. Ecuadorean province in the Oriente region. Prior to November 10, 1953, Morona-Santiago formed one province with Zamora-Chinchipe. Total area, 18,358 square miles. Separate area figures are unavailable. Population (1968 est.), 35,300.

MOSQUERA-GALDIANO AGREEMENT. Signed December 18, 1823, the boundaries are those fixed as of 1809 between the viceroyalties of Peru and New Granada. The signatories were Joaquín Mosquera y Arboleda for New Granada and José María Galdiano for Peru. This was the first of a long series of treaties or agreements designed to settle the boundary problems of what are now the nations of Ecuador, Colombia, and Peru; problems still not finally resolved.

MOSQUERA NARVAEZ, AURELIO. Born, August 2, 1883, Quito. Died, November 16, 1939, Quito. Education: M.D., Central University of Quito, 1906. Physician, politician; university professor, 1907-1912; deputy from Pichincha Province, 1914-15 and 1928-29; deputy from the same province and vice-president of the Chamber of Deputies 1930-31; vice-president of the Senate, 1935. Presidency: elected (Constituent Convention), age 55, 1938, one term; died in office, 1939.

MOSQUERA-PEDEMONTE TREATY   see   PEDEMONTE-
   MOSQUERA TREATY

MOSQUERA Y ARBOLEDA, ...   see   MOSQUERA-GALDIANO
   AGREEMENT

MOTE.   The Ecuadorean word for hominy, whether in the
   form generally known in the U. S., or as prepared or
   utilized in a great number of native dishes, both in
   the pealed form, and without removing the cuticle of
   the corn after soaking it in hot wood-lye or quick-
   lime solution.

MOURGEON, JUAN DE LA CRUZ.   Temporarily president
   of the Audiencia of Quito, December 1821, to April
   1822, when he died during the battles for independence.

MOVIMIENTO CIVICO DEMOCRATICO NACIONAL (MCDN).
   An ad-hoc coalition established in May, 1947, by in-
   dependent liberals who supported the candidacy of
   Galo Plaza Lasso in the 1948 presidential election.
   Plaza won the election.

MOVIMIENTO CIVICO INDEPENDIENTE   see   MOVIMIENTO
   FRENTE ...

MOVIMIENTO FRENTE POPULAR VELASQUISTA (MFPV).
   An ad-hoc coalition which supported the 1968 candi-
   dacies of José María Velasco Ibarra (president) and
   Victor Hugo Sicouret Pazmiño (vice-president).   The
   coalition was composed of the National Velasquista
   Federation (FNV) and partially by the popular Patriotic
   Party (PPP), and the Concentration of Popular Forces
   (CFP).   It was further supported by a host of ad-hoc
   movements, i. e. National Arosemenist Movement
   (MNA), Popular Liberation (LP), Independent Civic
   Movement (MCI), et al.   Velasco Ibarra won the
   election with almost 33% of the valid votes cast.

MOVIMIENTO NACIONAL AROSEMENISTA   see   MOVI-
   MIENTO NACIONAL REVOLUCIONARIO

MOVIMIENTO NACIONAL REVOLUCIONARIO (MNR).   A
   personalist political movement founded in February,
   1969.   It is headed by former President Carlos Julio
   Arosemena Monroy.   Previously it was known as the
   National Arosemenist Movement (MNA), which supported

the candidacy of José María Velasco Ibarra in the 1968
presidential election. The movement elected one
senator and four deputies in the 1968 congressional
elections. Its major strength is in Guayaquil and
among unionized labor. The Movement received official
recognition from the Supreme Electoral Tribunal in
1969 and is presently known as the Partido Nacional
Revolucionario (PNR).

MOVIMIENTO REPUBLICANO INDEPENDIENTE ECUATORI-
ANO (MRIE). A personalist movement founded by
Vicente Leví Castillo in 1961 as Movimiento Republicano Independiente (MRI). It is based in Guayaquil
and supported José María Velasco Ibarra in the 1968
presidential election. The movement elected one
deputy to the nation's Congress in 1968. The movement received official recognition from the Supreme
Electoral Tribunal in 1969 and is presently known as
the Partido Republicano Independiente (PRI).

MOVIMIENTO SOCIAL CRISTIANO (MSC). The Social
Christian Movement forms the moderate wing of the
conservative political elements. The party was
founded in 1951 by Camilo Ponce Enríquez, who continues to be its leader. The MSC enjoys the largest
support within the Conservative ranks including that
of the Catholic hierarchy. Although the MSC's following is heavily concentrated in the Sierra, Ponce
Enríquez drew a sizeable number of votes from the
Costa in the 1968 presidential election. When Ponce
Enríquez won the 1956 election he was and remains
the only president with a conservative background to
be elected to the presidency since 1895. In 1965,
the MSC organized its own youth movement in an
attempt to appeal to the younger sector; the movement is known as the Juventud Revolucionaria Social-
Christiana (JRSC).

MOYA. Quechuanism for a rather low, level area, or
meadow, fit for the raising of cattle. By extension,
a garden or orchard area.

MRI (also, MRIE)   see   MOVIMIENTO REPUBLICANO ...
(MRIE)

MSC   see   MOVIMIENTO SOCIAL CRISTIANO

MUNIVE Y ASPEE, LOPE ANTONIO DE. Born, Marquina,
1630. Died, Quito, 1689. Bachiller en cánones,
University of Salamanca. Public official. Magistrate
of the Audiencia of Lima, 1666; supervisor of the mines
of Huancavelica, 1674-76; president of the Audiencia of
Quito, January 29, 1678 until his death; Knight of the
Order of Alcántara and Marqués de Valdelirios.

MUÑOZ DE GUZMAN, LUIS ANTONIO. Public official.
Elected president of the Audiencia of Quito, March 25,
1790, he took office on June 30, 1791. Subsequently
he was sent to Chile (1798).

MUÑOZ-VERNAZA-SUAREZ TREATY. July 15, 1916.
Ecuador cedes about 200,000 square km. (80,000 sq.
mi.) in the Putumayo and Caquetá regions to Colombia.
The same territory was ceded by Colombia to Peru in
1922 (Salamón-Lozano Treaty, March 24, 1922).

MURILLO MIRO, JUAN. Born, ca.1850, Guayaquil. Died,
1895?, Guayaquil. Historian and journalist.

MUSHPA. Quechua term, generally, but used by Spanish-
speakers also, to mean fool or imbecile.

- N -

ÑAÑA. Originally a Quechua feminine noun form meaning
sister. A masculine form, ñaño, has been invented
and means brother. (The initial ñ has the sound of
the internal ñ.)

ÑAÑERIA. From the preceding word, comes this expression, a noun meaning familiarity, camaraderie,
brotherly relationship.

NAPO. Northernmost Ecuadorean province in the Oriente
region. Prior to October 22, 1959, Napo formed with
Pastaza one province. Separate area figures are unavailable. Population (1968 est.), 33,600.

NAPO. An archeological site located on the eastern slopes
of the Andes along the Napo river. The site dates
back to A.D. 1100's. Little is known of the phase and
few artifacts have been associated with it outside of
pottery.

NARVAEZ, DIEGO DE. Born, Antequera. Died, Quito,
1581. Public official. Appointed magistrate of
Panama, 1569, but declined; magistrate of Bogotá,
1569; and Lima, 1574. President of the Audiencia
of Quito, June 2, 1578. Died in office.

NEBOT VELASCO, JAIME. Born, December 28, 1921,
Guayaquil. Education: Law, University of Guayaquil,
1946. Lawyer, politician, economist. Public service:
governor of Guayas Province; minister of Economics,
1954; minister of Agriculture; minister of Development,
1961.

NEUMAN, GITI. Born, March 25, 1941, Prague. Contemporary painter who has exhibited widely, including
a one artist show at the Pan American Union, 1966.
She studied at the Escuela de Bellas Artes, Quito,
and with Lloyd Wulf, Alberto Coloma Silva, Jaime
Valencia. Secretary of the Asociación de Artes
Plásticas.

NEUMANNE, ANTONIO. Born, June 13, 1818, Corsica (of
German parents). Died, March 3, 1871, Quito. Education: Musical conservatory in Milan, Italy. Musi-
cian. Public service: came to Ecuador in 1841 as
director of the opera company and settled there perma-
nently in 1851. He established the Conservatory of
Music in Quito, 1870; composed the national anthem
which was declared official by the Congress of 1866.

NEVAREZ VASQUEZ, ROBERTO. Born, November 14, 1911,
Guayaquil. Education: M. D. , Guayaquil. Physician.
Public service: governor of Guayas province; minister
of Social Welfare and Health. Vice-presidential running
mate of Camilo Ponce Enríquez in the 1968 national
election.

NINACURO. Quechuan term for the fire-fly.

NIZA, MARCOS DE. Born, about 1500, Nice. Died, after
1543, probably in Mexico. Franciscan priest and
explorer. Writer. Fray Marcos de Niza was with
Benalcázar at the founding of the Spanish city of Quito
in 1534. Afterward he led the exploring expedition
northward from Mexico City in 1539 which discovered
Arizona. His Cartas informativas de lo obrado en las
provincias del Perú y de Quito, and Las dos líneas de

los incas y de los scyris en las provincias del Perú
y de Quito are important early writings about Ecuador.

NOBOA CAAMAÑO, ERNESTO.   Born 1892, Quito; died 1928.
Modernist poet.

NOBOA Y ARTETA, DIEGO.   Born, October 15, 1789,
Guayaquil.   Died, November 3, 1870, Guayaquil.   One
of the triumvirate which formed a liberal government
on March 6, 1845, when Juan José Flores was overthrown.   After a new constitution was adopted Noboa
succeeded to the presidency in 1850, but was overthrown the next year.

NUEVA GRANADA.   Name applied before Independence to
the area now comprising Venezuela, Colombia, Ecuador,
and Panama, a viceroyalty after 1718 and 1740.

NUEVO SUCESO.   Monthly magazine of political content published in Guayaquil.   First issued on December 14,
1961, it has a circulation of 12,000.   Its editorial
policy is independent and its director is Eduardo Ca-
prión Puertas.

- O -

OBRAJES.   Work center where Indians are employed to
make felt hats and weave woolen cloth.

OCEPA   see next entry

OFICINA CENTRAL DE EXPORTACION DE PRODUCTOS
ARTESANALES (OCEPA).   Central Office for the
Exportation of Popular Crafts.   OCEPA has two major
objectives: a) to improve the quality of workmanship
and design of popular craft products, and b) to find
export markets for the same.

OILFIELDS.   Ecuador was for a time at least relatively
self sufficient in petroleum needs through the exploitation of the Ancón deposits on the Santa Elena Peninsula.   With the discovery of oil east of the Andes in
the Lago Agrío region and elsewhere, some 15 con-
cessions to foreign companies have been approved, and
a new oilduct, 318 miles in length, across the Andes
to the port of Esmeraldas has been completed, making

the country an important exporter of petroleum. A
government oil corporation and resource authority,
the Corporación Estatal Petrolera Ecuatoriana, was
established in 1971. In 1972 sale of petroleum
abroad should be equivalent to 35 per cent of the export income.

OJOTA [also, Oxota, oshota, ushuta, shota]. Quechuanism
for a type of simple sandal consisting of a sole of
twisted vegetable cord or rope with a thong to hold
it on the foot of the wearer, like some of the Mexican
huraches.

OLEAS ZAMBRANO, GONZALO. Born, February 16, 1916,
Riobamba. Education: Law, Central University of
Quito. Lawyer, politician. Deputy, leader of the
Ecuadorean Socialist Party (PSE), and its most in-
fluential member from Quito.

OLMEDO, JOSE JOAQUIN. Born, March 19, 1780, Guayaquil. Died, February 17, 1847, Guayaquil. Education: Law, Colegio San Carlos, Lima, Peru. Lawyer, poet, publicist. Vice-president of the Republic;
prefect of Guayas Province, 1830. Olmedo played an
instrumental role in the struggle for independence
from Spain. He was a member of the triumvirate of
liberals which overthrew Juan José Flores, March 6,
1845. His poetry is very highly regarded and frequently recited even today.

ORDOÑEZ, JOSE IGNACIO. Born, Cuenca, July 21, 1829.
Died, Quito, July 14, 1893. Clergyman. Bishop of
Riobamba; Ecuadorean plenipotentiary to the Vatican
for the signing of the 1862 Concordat, which was
ratified by President Gabriel García Moreno a year
later; sixth archbishop of Quito, 1882-93.

ORELLANA, FRANCISCO DE. Born, 1511, Trujillo, Spain.
Died, November 10, 1546, probably in what is today
Venezuela. One of Gonzalo Pizarro's captains, who
participated in the expedition from Quito eastward
across the Andes, 1540-41. He left Pizarro and
continued the journey from the Napo river to the
Valley of the Amazon, exploring the course of the
river from the Andes to the Atlantic Ocean, 1542.
He returned to the Amazon basin with his own expedition in 1544 in the hope of establishing a colony but

failed and died soon thereafter.

ORELLANA POZO, J. GONZALO. Born, July 16, 1904,
Cuenca. Education: University of Azuay, Law. Politician, historian. Governor of Azuay Province; Intendant General of Police; author: Resumen histórico
del Ecuador, 2 vols., 1948.

ORIENTE. Comprises the area east of the Eastern Cordillera including its slopes and the lush jungle of the
Amazon basin. The Oriente covers approximately
56,000 square miles or about one half of the national
territory. Politically the Oriente is divided into four
provinces: Morona-Santiago, Napo, Pastaza, and
Zamora-Chinchipe. It is in this region that proven oil
wells have been developed, with a pipeline to carry the
petroleum over the Andes.

ORTIZ GARCES, HUGO. Born, August 5, 1921, Guayaquil.
Died, August 5, 1941, Santiago. Lieutenant in the
Ecuadorean army stationed in the Oriente Province
when the area was invaded by the Peruvian army,
August 2, 1941. Killed in action, he was proclaimed
a national hero and decorated posthumously.

ORTIZ QUIÑONES, ADALBERTO. Born, February 9, 1914,
Esmeraldas. Educated at the Juan Montalvo College
as a teacher. Widely acclaimed novelist and poet who
has won several national prizes for his works. Author:
Juyungo, 1943; Tierra, son y tambor, 1945; La mala
espalda, 1952; El animal herido, 1961; El espejo y la
ventana, 1967.

OVIEDO Y VALDEZ ... see FERNANDEZ DE OVIEDO
Y VALDEZ ...

- P -

PAEZ, FEDERICO. Born, June 6, 1876, Quito. Education:
Ecole Superieur des Mines (Paris), 1895-97; Ecole
des Hautes Etudes Sociales (Brussels), 1900. Civil
engineer, politician. Civil engineer in Quito and
Guayaquil, 1913-18; deputy from Pichincha Province,
1916-18; Senator, 1932-35; Minister of Public Works,
1935; Professor of Geophysics in Costa Rica, 1940-
43. Presidency: non-elected, age 59, 1935, put in

power by the armed forces; ruled as a dictator and
relinquished power to General Alberto Enríquez Gallo
in 1937.

PAJA.   The generic word in Spanish for straw, but con-
textually in Ecuador it usually refers to the toquilla
or fine dried and bleached leaves of the plant (Carlu-
duvica palmata) used in the making of "Panama" hats.
See JIPIJAPA.

PAJA BRAVA.   Coarse grass which grows on the Andean
plateaus (páramos).   Used for thatch and fuel.

PALTA.   The Palta and Malacato were aboriginal tribes
that occupied Loja Province and partially the provinces
of El Oro and Jaén (present-day Peru).   Because both
tribes readily submitted to the Inca conquest little
is known about them.

PALTA.   Quechuan name for the aguacate or what is called
avocado in the United States.

PAMPA.   This Quechuan word is familiar in Argentina,
meaning plain or flatland.   In the Andean area it
appears in many place names; in this same spelling
or in the form bamba--Tomebamba, Riobamba, etc.

PANAMA HATS.   High-grade straw hats which are a major
export item.   The "Panama" hat industry is centered
in the towns of Montecristi and Jipijapa in Manabí
Province.   See JIPIJAPA.   Cuenca is also a major
production center.

PANDO-NOBOA TREATY.   July 12, 1832.   Signed with
Peru.   Established an alliance which served to unite
the two nations in the period of the 1866 effort of
Spain to re-conquer the Viceroyalty of Peru.

PANZALEO.   An Indian tribe that lived in Pichincha,
Cotopaxi and Tungurahua provinces at the time of
the Spanish conquest.

PARAMO.   High, treeless plains of the Andean region,
usually windswept.

PAREDES, DIOGENES.   Born, 1910, Quito.   Died, 1969(?),
Quito.   School of Fine Arts, Quito.   Internationally

known painter. The exhibition gallery in the Casa de
la Cultura Ecuatoriana in Quito is named for him.

PAREDES, MARIANA DE JESUS (SANTA). Born, October 31,
 1618, Quito. Died, May 26, 1645, Quito. Child of
 Doña Mariana Granobles Jaramillo and Captain Jerón-
 imo Flores Zenel de Paredes, the former a native of
 Quito and the latter, of Toledo, Spain. Beatified,
 October 7, 1850 at Rome. Sanctified, July 9, 1950.

PAREJA, JUAN IGNACIO. Born, Guayaquil. Died, 1838,
 Guayaquil. Naval captain and soldier. In the Spanish
 navy he held the rank of frigate captain, and in the
 Ecuadorean army, that of general. He took part in
 various engagements during the wars of independence,
 including the Battle of Pichincha, and later served as
 prefect of Guayaquil (1830), and in similar governmental activities.

PAREJA DIEZCANSECO, ALFREDO. Born, October 12,
 1908, Guayaquil. Educated at the Central University
 of Quito, secondary education in history. Professor.
 One of the best and most prolific Ecuadorean novelists,
 he has also written a history of Ecuador and a biography
 of Eloy Alfaro titled: La hoguera bárbara, 1944.
 Pareja Diezcanseco has also served as a leader of the
 liberally oriented Democratic National Front in 1956
 and 1960, and as visiting professor in various universities in the United States. Most important novels:
 El muelle, 1933; La beldaca, 1935; Baldomera, 1938;
 Hechos y hazañas de Don Balón de Baba y de su amigo
 Inocente Cruz, 1939; Hombres sin tiempo, 1941; Los
 nueve años, 2 vols., 1956-59. Presently serving as
 assistant general manager of the Banco Popular in
 Guayaquil.

PARRA VELASCO, ANTONIO. Born, 1900, Guayaquil.
 Education: J.D., University of Guayaquil. Lawyer,
 politician, diplomat. Public service: minister of
 Foreign Relations and Education, unsuccessful presidential candidate for a left-wing coalition in 1960.

PARROQUIA. Although the word means parish or parish
 church, the smallest ecclesiastical unit in all Spain
 and Spanish speaking countries, in Ecuador it is used
 to designate the smallest civil administrative unit in
 the national government. It is presided over by a

teniente político or political deputy. The cura (parish
priest) controls the ecclesiastical unit.

PARTIDARIO. Term used to define an individual who serves
as sponsor or backer of share croppers.

PARTIDO COMUNISTA ECUATORIANO (PCE). The Communist Party was formally organized in 1928. The
founder, Dr. Ricardo Paredes, was unsuccessful in
his attempt to recruit from among the Indians of the
Sierra and turned toward support among the urban
proletariat. In addition to an intellectual following the
PCE controls Ecuador's largest labor federation, the
Confederation of Ecuadorean Workers (CTE). The
PCE is divided into Moscow-Peking-Cuba factions of
which the former is the most important. The secretary general of the Party since 1944 has been Pedro
Saad, who also often served as functional senator of
Labor from the coast. While the Party is unconsti-
tutional, it has been allowed to operate in the open
with exception of the days of the military junta (1963-
66). In the 1968 presidential election, the PCE
organized its own coalition movement, the Popular
Democratic Union (UDP). Its candidates were Elías
Gallegos Anda (president) and Gonzalo Villalba (vice-
president). Both finished a distant last in a five-
man field with about 2 percent of the valid votes cast.

PARTIDO CONSERVADOR (PC). Conservative Party,
founded 1869, and recognized as one of the official
traditional political parties by the Constitution of 1945.
It caters nowadays largely to elitist interests.

PARTIDO DEMOCRATA-CRISTIANO (PDC). The Christian
Democratic Party was organized in 1965 with the
ostensible object of duplicating the success of Eduardo
Frei in Chile. Little is known of the party's strength
as it did not support a candidate in the 1968 presidential election. In the 1968 congressional election the
PDC elected one senator and one deputy both of whom
were evicted from the party in 1969.

PARTIDO LIBERAL-RADICAL (PLR). The PLR was officially organized in 1878 by Ignacio de Veintimilla and
held its first General Assembly in 1890. The party
came to power with the 1895 revolution of Eloy Alfaro
and ruled almost uninterruptedly until 1944. The Party

is responsible for separating church and state (1906)
and the introduction of public education.   In the past
25 years the party has been too weak to elect its own
candidate in presidential contests, and has formed
coalitions with parties of center left orientation.

PARTIDO NACIONAL REVOLUCIONARIO see MOVIMIENTO
    NACIONAL ...

PARTIDO PATRIOTICO POPULAR (PPP).   Initially known
    as Partido Patriótico Nacional (PPN).   A conservative
    group which broke away from the Conservative Party
    in 1966 under the leadership of the now deceased
    Ruperto Alarcón Falconi.   The PPP supported José
    María Velasco Ibarra in the 1968 presidential election.
    It decided to run its own candidates for the legislature,
    but elected none.

PARTIDO REPUBLICANO INDEPENDIENTE (PRI) [also,
    ... ECUATORIANO (PRIE)] see MOVIMIENTO
    REPUBLICANO ...

PARTIDO SOCIALISTA ECUATORIANO (PSE).   The Socialist
    Party of Ecuador was formally founded in May, 1926,
    although various socialist clubs had existed since 1922.
    It draws its support from students and intellectuals and
    has enjoyed varied success.   Socialist deputies were
    instrumental in drafting the never promulgated 1938
    constitution.   The Party also enjoyed some power
    during the government of Alberto Enríquez Gallo (1937-
    38) and Galo Plaza Lasso (1948-52).   The PSE is
    presently divided into various factions.   The most
    prominent are led by Dr. Gonzalo Oleas Zambrano,
    a Quito lawyer, and, in Cuenca, by Dr. Carlos Cueva
    Tamáriz.   The latter group calls itself "Socialismo
    Unificado."   The split appears to be more personal
    than ideological.

PARTIDO SOCIALISTA REVOLUCIONARIO ECUATORIANO
    (PSRE).   A political movement which broke away from
    the PSE in 1962.   It is most readily identifiable with
    the PCE.   The present leader of the PSRE is Aníbal
    Muñoz.   The party elected one deputy in the 1968
    congressional election.

PASTAZA.   Ecuadorean province in the Oriente region.
    Prior to October 22, 1959, Pastaza formed with Napo

one province.   Separate area figures are not available.
Population (1968 est.), 19,000.

PATRON. General term for any one who hires the work of
others, but specifically the patron of Indian clients in
any activity, usually agricultural.   Clever Indian and
mestizo clients know how to exploit the patrón as well
as to protect themselves against him.

PATRONATO REAL. "Royal patronage" granted by Pope
Alexander VI to the kings of Spain, under which they
controlled church appointments in the colonies in
perpetuity.

PAZ Y MIÑO, GERMANIA. Born, December 15, 1916,
Quito.   Educated, Colegio de la Providencia and
National School of Fine Arts, Quito.   Painter and
sculptress.   Professor of drawing and painting in
the "Peres Pallares" Institute in Quito, and in the
National School of Fine Arts.   Her works are in
numerous public and private collections and public
monuments.   Writer and art critic, El Comercio, Quito.
A long time resident of New York.

PAZ Y MIÑO, LUIS TELMO. Born, April 15, 1884, Quito.
Soldier, educator, man of letters.   He occupied various charges in the military, including that of director
of the Military Academy and Chief of Staff.   First
president of the military junta, June 9, 1925.   Professor of Cartography and Geography.   Founder of the
Geographic Society of Quito.

PC   see   PARTIDO CONSERVADOR

PCE   see   PARTIDO COMUNISTA ECUATORIANO

PCN   see   POLICIA CIVIL NACIONAL

PDC   see   PARTIDO DEMOCRATA-CRISTIANO

PEDEMONTE-MOSQUERA PROTOCOL.   Agreement signed
August 11, 1830 in Lima by General Tomás Cipriano
Mosquera, ambassador of Gran Colombia, and José
Pedemonte, minister for Foreign Affairs of Peru.
This protocol was intended not as a separate treaty,
but merely as the written statement concerning the
implementation of the terms on the boundary between

Gran Colombia and Peru as stated in the Treaty of
Guayaquil, September 2, 1829. Because of both the
eventual separation of Ecuador, Colombia, and Venezuela into three nations--fragmenting the original Gran
Colombia--and Ecuador's ignorance of the signing of
the protocol (its contents were not revealed until 1904,
when the Colombian Embassy in Lima made a certified copy available to the Ecuadorean Embassy), it
never was put into effect. Its importance lies in the
fact that it fixes the Marañón River as the boundary
between the two countries, beginning at its confluence
with the Amazon and proceeding upstream to the confluence of the Chinchipe River, and across the watershed to the Túmbez River and thence to the Pacific
Ocean. This would have assured Ecuador of direct
access to the Amazon River and a vast territory now
known to include extensive petroleum deposits would
have remained a part of her territory. Peruvian armed
invasion reduced Ecuador to her present much more
limited area, and a greatly reduced portion of the petroleum bearing lands.

PEÑAHERRERA, VICTOR MANUEL. Born, 1864, Ibarra.
Died, 1932, Quito. Educated at the Central University
in Quito, J. D. Lawyer. He served as minister of
State and president of the Supreme Court. As a professor of law he wrote several textbooks, and he was
the author of the basic labor law of Ecuador.

PEÑA Y MONTENEGRO, ALONSO DE. Born, Villa del
Padrón, Galicia, Spain. Died, May 12, 1688, Quito.
Educated at the University of Santiago de Compostela.
Professor there and at Salamanca. Author of works
on missionary methods which contain much material
of anthropological interest. During his presidency the
volcano, Pichincha, erupted so violently and extensively
that ashes fell from Popayán to Loja. President of
the Audiencia of Quito, 1674-1678.

PEPA DE ORO. Name given to the cacao bean which provided the major source of income for the nation during
the cacao boom of 1894-1905.

PEREZ CASTRO, FRANCISCO. Born, 1908?, Guayaquil.
Educated Colegio Juan Montalvo and Colegio Vicente
Rocafuerte. Newspaperman, poet. Editor, El Uni-
verso. Member of various cultural and learned

societies.   Brother of Ismael Pérez Castro, and a co-founder of El Universo.

PEREZ CASTRO, ISMAEL.   Born, September 30, 1902, Machala.   Died, February 24, 1967, Guayaquil. Founder and publisher of Ecuador's largest daily newspaper, El Universo of Guayaquil.

PEREZ CONCHA, JORGE.   Born, June 5, 1908, Guayaquil. Educated at the University of Guayaquil.   Historian, newspaperman, educator.   Publisher of the evening daily, La Razón, Guayaquil.   Member of various learned and scientific societies, he has been prominent in international gatherings.   He has occupied a number of diplomatic posts and has served in the ministry of Public Education.   Biographer of Eloy Alfaro, Luis Vargas Torres, etc. and author of a treatise on Ecuadorean relations with bordering nations.

PEREZ DE SALAZAR, ALONSO.   Died, 1642.   Public official.   President of the Audiencia of Quito, 1637-42.   Died on his way to assume the presidency of the Audiencia of Charcas.

PEREZ FEBRES CORDERO, FRANCISCO.   Born, Guayaquil. Education: B. A. in Journalism, University of Miami, Fla.   Newspaperman, poet.   He has published several books of poetry, and writes for a number of Ecuadorean newspapers.   He is considered one of the leading present-day poets of Ecuador and Spanish America, with international recognition.

PERU.   Ecuador's neighboring nation to the south.   After the conquest of Peru (1531-1535), all of the Spanish holdings in South America were included under the Viceroyalty of Peru, with subdivision into audiencias headed by a presidente, as at Quito, from 1563.   In the 18th century new viceroyalties were established at Buenos Aires, for the Río de la Plata, and in the north at Caracas, for New Granada, to include what are now Colombia, Venezuela, Panama, and Ecuador. Jurisdictions in the area which was later to become the Republic of Ecuador were rather clearcut until the Cédula of 1802, when a large portion of the southeastern trans-Andean region, known as Mainas and Quijos, occupied from Quito only in the institution of mission establishments among the indigenous population,

was reassigned to the jurisdiction of the church in
Lima. Although the Peruvians, upon winning independence, agreed in 1829--in the Treaty of Guayaquil
(Larrea-Gual Treaty)--to the boundaries of 1810,
defining them as they were prior to the Cédula de
1802, subsequent modifications in claims based on the
latter, and on other arguments, led to the Protocol of
Rio de Janeiro in 1942, which has resulted in the still
disputed eastern boundary of Ecuador. The repeated
efforts at settlement are listed under the various
treaty entries in this Dictionary.

PICHINCHA.   A dormant volcano located on the northwestern skirts of Quito.   Pichincha (meaning: "boil-
ing mountain") has an elevation of 15,918 feet.   Its
crater measures nearly a mile across and is 2500
feet deep.   Violent eruptions in 1539, 1577, 1587,
and 1660 and at other times in the colonial period
wrought serious damage and many inhabitants of Quito
and vicinity were killed.

PICHINCHA.   A province in Ecuador located in the highlands and named after the volcano Pichincha.   Total
land area is 5976 square miles.   The national capital,
Quito, is also the capital of the province.   Population (1968 est.),   761,100.

PICHINCHA, BATTLE OF.   May 24, 1822.   The Spanish
forces under General Melchor Aymerich were defeated
by the patriotic forces under General Sucre assuring
the independence of Ecuador.   May 24 is a national
holiday in Ecuador.

PIEDRAHITA, VICENTE.   Born, June 22, 1833, Guayaquil.   Died, September 4, 1878, near Daule, Guayas
Province.   Statesman.   Commercial envoy in Chile,
1860; Governor of Guayas Province, 1862-64; Minister
Plenipotentiary in Peru, 1868-73.   One of the most
important Ecuadorean diplomats of the 19th century
who represented his country in many international conferences.   He was assassinated at his hacienda, La
Palestina, due to his opposition to the Veintimilla
government and his connection with Eloy Alfaro and
other young opponents of the former.

PIFANO.   A kind of native fife, made of reed, and with
six holes, as opposed to the three in the pinguillo,
another flutelike instrument.

PILADA. The process of threshing and polishing of rice. (From the verb, pilar, an alternate form of pelar, to peal or remove the husk from grain, fruit, or vegetables.) The word is, however, employed because of the pila (pilón) or mortar in which the grain was placed to be struck with a wooden pestle to remove the husk.

PILADORA. Storage place and processing plant where rice is threshed and polished. See PILADA

PINGANILLAS. In the 18th century, vendors in the public markets. Also a disdainful term used to refer to persons of uncertain birth and origin who attempted to enter the upper class. Equivalent of the present day chulla, q. v.

PINTAC. One of the most able generals of Cacha Scyri XV, who ruled the kingdom of Quito from 1463-87. When the latter's armies were defeated by the Inca Huayna-Cápac at the battle of Caranquí, Pintac managed to escape with some of his troops and continue harassment of the Inca forces. Eventually captured, he refused to subordinate himself to the Inca ruler and died while on a hunger strike. It is said that Huayna-Cápac, whose respect Pintac had earned, wanted to keep his fame alive and, consequently, ordered that a drum be made of his skin. This drum was used in Cuzco during the festivities of Inti-Raimi, a celebration in honor of the sun.

PINTO, JOAQUIN. Born, August 18, 1842, Quito. Died, June 14, 1906, Quito. A leading Ecuadorean painter of the 19th century, he studied with Nicolás Cabrera and contemporaries. Largely self-taught in some areas of his artistic activity, he learned several modern and the classic languages and taught in the schools of fine arts both in Quito and Cuenca. He effectively introduced the Ecuadorean Indian as subject of artistic inspiration.

PIRCA. Commonly used in rural areas to mean wall, fence, or enclosing structure. In the case of ingapirca, as in other place names, it refers to any ruin or structural remains.

PITI. Native word for a small quantity, very little in amount.

PIZARRO, GONZALO. Born, 1506, Trujillo (Cáceres),

Spain. Died, April 12, 1548, Cuzco. Brother of
Francisco, with whom he participated in the conquest
of Peru. Appointed governor of Quito in 1539, he
was charged with the exploration of the Andean region
of the headwaters of the Amazon. His lieutenant,
Francisco de Orellana, was placed in charge of the
exploration of navigable waters and completed the
journey coastward to the Atlantic. Gonzalo returned
to Quito from the Napo area in 1542 to find that his
brother had been assassinated. In the political chaos
and rebellions which followed, his transgressions in
the power structure brought about his capture and
execution for treason.

PIZARRO, PEDRO. Born, ca. 1499, Spain. Died, February 9, 1587. Chronicler, historian. First cousin
of Francisco Pizarro. Early historian of the Presidency of Quito.

PLAZA GUTIERREZ, LEONIDAS. Born, April 18, 1865,
Charapotó, Manabí Province. Died, September 18,
1932, Huigra, Tungurahua Province. Education:
military. Military career, politician, Sergeant major,
1884; major general in Costa Rica, 1893; governor of
Azuay Province, 1896; commander-in-chief of the
coastal provinces and of the coastal army, 1900;
deputy from Tungurahua Province and president of
the Chamber of Deputies, 1900-1901; minister of
Finance, 1911; deputy from Esmeraldas Province,
1911; chief of staff of the Armed Forces, 1911-12.
Presidency: (1) elected (popular), age 36, 1901,
one term, which ended constitutionally in 1905;
(2) elected (popular), age 47, 1912, one term, which
ended constitutionally in 1916.

PLAZA LASSO, GALO. Born, February 17, 1906, New
York. Son of the preceding. Education: University
of Maryland, 1929. Georgetown School of Foreign
Affairs, 1930. Gentleman farmer, politician, diplomat; civil attaché in the Ecuadorean Legation in Washington, 1929; member of Quito Municipal Council, 1937;
minister of National Defense, 1938-40; ambassador to
the United States, 1944-46; senator from Pichincha
Province, 1946; United Nations representative in Cyprus,
1964; secretary general of the OAS, 1967. Presidency:
elected (popular), age 42, 1946, one term, completed
in 1952.

PLR see PARTIDO LIBERAL-RADICAL

POLICIA CIVIL NACIONAL (PCN). The National Civil
Police.

POLIT LASO, MANUEL MARIA. Born, March 25, 1865,
Quito. Died, October 28, 1932, Quito. Education:
Doctor of Theology. Clergyman, lawyer, teacher,
historian. Archbishop of Quito; taught at Central
University; founder of the Anales de la Universidad
de Quito. His extensive bibliography includes 309
different titles.

POLITICAL PARTIES. The right to organize politically,
provided that the political organization is guided by
democratic norms, is guaranteed by the 1946 constitution. At present, Ecuador has a multiparty system
composed of officially recognized parties and extra-
legal parties. Official recognition is granted by the
Supreme Electoral Tribunal (TSE). In 1970 there
were 12 official parties and a host of extralegal
political parties most of which are temporary in nature.
Of the 12 official parties, five can be considered conservative in orientation (ARNE, PC, PPP, MSC, CID);
six are taken to be liberal and/or moderate (PLR,
FNV, CTP, PNR, PRIE, PSE), and one leftist in
orientation (UDP). The most important extralegal
movements are the moderate PDC, MNR, PRI, and
the leftist PSRE and PCE. Most of the parties are
also characterized by a strong personalistic leadership.

POLIVIO CHAVES, ANGEL. Born, February 22, 1855,
Guaranda. Died, September 11, 1930, Guaranda.
Education: J.D., University of Quito. Journalist,
lawyer, military man. Founder of many periodicals
and newspapers, including Los Principios (January 18,
1883), which is considered the first daily to appear
in Quito.

PONCE BORJA, NICOLAS. Born, June 22, 1866. Quito.
Died, November 21, 1929, Panama. Education: J.D.,
University of Quito. Diplomat, lawyer. Served his
country as representative on boundary commissions;
wrote Limites entre el Ecuador y Perú.

PONCE-CASTRO-OYANGUREN PROTOCOL. June 21, 1924.

Provided that Ecuador and Peru should begin direct
negotiations in Washington over their boundary differences. In the event that such negotiations should fail,
the two governments should determine by common
accord the zones mutually recognized by each of the
parties and those which should be submitted to the
arbitral decision of the President of the United States.

PONCE ENRIQUEZ, CAMILO. Born, January 31, 1912, Quito.
Education: J. D. , Central University of Quito, 1938.
Lawyer, politician. Minister of Foreign Relations,
1952; head and founder of the Social Christian Movement, 1951. Presidency: elected (popular) age 44,
1956, one term, which ended constitutionally in 1960.

PONDO. A kind of large earthenware jar. Persons whose
rotund stature warrants it are likely to be nicknamed
"pondo. "

PONS, ANTONIO. Born, November 10, 1897. Education:
M. D. , Diplomat, physician. Minister of the Interior,
1934. Presidency: non-elected. Replaced José
María Velasco Ibarra in 1935, and handed over the
reins of government to the military after having been
in office less than a month, August 21 to September
26.

POPULATION. November 1971 figures of the National
Statistical Institute give 6, 284, 000 as total inhabitants,
of which 3, 900, 543 are rural, and 2, 483, 657 urban.
Guayaquil had 835, 812 and Quito, 551, 163, inhabitants.
58 per cent of the population is under 20 years of
age. Other cities of more than 50, 000 are: Cuenca,
Ambato, Machala, Esmeraldas, and Riobamba.

POROTO. Native word for beans of various types. Used
as a nickname for persons of small, delicate stature.

PORTEÑO. A resident of the coastal city of Guayaquil.

PORTETE. Minor mountain pass. Ecuadorian usage.

PORTETE DE TARQUI see TARQUI

PORTOVIEJO. Capital of the Province of Manabí. Population (1968 est.), 50, 000.

PPP [also, PPN] see PARTIDO PATRIOTICO POPULAR

LA PRENSA. Guayaquil daily, late-edition paper with a
    circulation of 5000. It was founded in 1923 and has
    an independent editorial policy. Its director is
    Pompilio Ulloa Reyes.

PRESIDENTE. Head of a village council (cabildo) under the
    system of comunas.

PRESIDENTS. Under the constitution of Ecuador the presi-
    dency is to be filled by direct vote of all male and
    female electors. The president is to serve a four-
    year term, and he may not be re-elected except after
    one term out of office. Nevertheless, this general
    rule has not always been followed, some presidents
    having been elected by the indirect vote of the Congress
    or in other ways. (See CONSTITUTIONS.) In the
    years of Ecuador's existence as an independent nation
    (1830-1972), 51 different individuals have occupied the
    presidency, as a result of 84 turnovers giving an
    average term of office of less than 1 1/2 years.
    (See Appendix 7.) Provisional juntas have governed
    the country during a total of about four years and
    three months out of the total of 152 years. Not in-
    cluded in the total are the individuals who served
    only briefly during the time of an incumbent's incapa-
    citation or absence from the country. Of the 51 presi-
    dents, only Flores, Urbina, Veintimilla, Alfaro,
    Plaza Gutiérrez, and Rodríguez Lara have been career
    military men. Of the total, 40 have had university
    training, and 22 have held a doctorate in law or medi-
    cine. Only 15 of the elected presidents have served
    out a full term, however. Seventy-four per cent of
    the presidents had been members of Congress prior
    to occupying the Presidency, and 52 per cent had been
    Cabinet Officers. Until 1895 all occupants were con-
    sidered of conservative political beliefs, and since
    that time all but Ponce Enríquez have been Liberals or
    Radical Liberals. A complete list of the presidents
    and their terms of office appears in this work as
    Appendix 7, as well as a brief biographical summary
    of each, and an indication as to the manner whereby
    he reached the office, elected or non-elected.

PRI[E] see MOVIMIENTO REPUBLICANO ...

PRIMICIA.   First fruits, collected by the church as a
privilege levy.

PRIOSTE.   An Indian official in the highland area selected
by the parish and charged with the duty of supervising
a fiesta.   The latter may be religious or civic in nature.   In religious fiestas the prioste has to bear the
expenses for food or drink.   Considerable prestige is
associated with this office and all adult males of the
Indian community are expected to assume this function
at some time.

PROAÑO, FEDERICO.   Born, Cuenca, March 14, 1848.
Died, Quetzaltenango, Guatemala, May 22, 1894.
Educated for the priesthood, which he abandoned to
become founder of a newspaper in company with
Miguel Valverde, in opposition to García Moreno at
Guayaquil, La Nueva Era.   Forced into exile he
reached Lima, Peru, then continued on to Central
America, after a short time in Ecuador when García
Moreno was assassinated.   He was a writer of no
small talent and much has been written of his career.

PROGRESISMO.   A coalition movement of Conservatives
and Radical liberals which had its heydey during the
1890's.

PROTOCOL OF RIO DE JANEIRO   see   RIO JANEIRO ...

PROVINCIA.   Political division corresponding to a U.S.
state.   There are 19 plus the Archipiélago de Colón,
or Galápagos Islands.   The provinces, with the capitals, are listed in Appendix 8 by their regional classi-
fication north to south.

PSE   see   PARTIDO SOCIALISTA ECUATORIANO

PSRE   see   PARTIDO SOCIALISTA REVOLUCIONARIO ...

PUCHO.   Quechua word for the butt or unsmoked portion
of a cigarette.

PUÑA.   An Indian tribe which inhabited the islands of the
same name situated near the southern coast of Ecuador.
The Puñá were successful as pirates and traders.
Early Spanish chroniclers were much impressed with
their prosperity.

PURO. From the Quechua puru, which means hollow, or
    empty, comes this word used to designate a kind of
    wooden vessel of native use and manufacture.

PURUHA. An Indian tribe that lived in Chimborazo and
    Bolívar provinces, south of the Panzaleo. The
    Puruhá were one of the most powerful highland tribes.
    After joining forces with the Caras (q. v.) they formed
    part of the Kingdom of Quito which lasted from 1300-
    1487 when the Incas conquered them. Also spelled
    Purujá.

PURUHA. Archeological site located in Riobamba basin,
    Central highlands. Named after the Puruhá tribe,
    the phase dates between A. D. 500 and 1500. The
    most characteristic remnants are anthropomorphic
    vessels.

PUTUMAYO RIVER. A tributary of the Amazon river which
    forms part of Ecuador's border with Colombia. Im-
    portant oil findings were made in 1966 near both banks.
    They already have raised the economic level of both
    countries.

PUYO. Capital of the province of Pastaza. Population
    (1968 est.) was less then 10, 000.

PUZUN. Native word widely used to mean the abdomen or
    belly of either man or beast.

- Q -

QUECHUA. The name given to the people and to the lan-
    guage of the Incan region (modern Peru and Southern
    Ecuador). Often spelled quichua in Ecuador. The
    Incas were so determined to make Quechua the sole
    language that they dispersed non-Quechuan tribes and
    moved Quechua-speaking people into the territories
    they conquered. See MITIMAES. Kichwa is an addi-
    tional transliteration employed by some students and
    scholars.

QUENA. Native flute.

QUEVEDO TORO, ALBERTO. Born, December 19, 1931,
    Quito. Education: J. D. , Central University, Quito;

M. S., public and private finance, Harvard University.
Economist and diplomat. He has occupied a number of
positions on international commissions, including the
Economic Commission for Latin America (CEPAL),
World Bank, and in national finance, such as that of
technical director of the Exchange Commission of the
National Finance Corporation, subsecretary of Commerce and Banking, and minister of Finance. He
was serving as manager of the newspaper publishing
firm, El Comercio, when named ambassador extraordinary and plenipotentiary to the United States on
September 1, 1972.

QUIJOS. Settlement founded by Egidio Ramírez Dávalos,
brother of Gil, on the eastern slopes of the Andes,
in 1562.

QUILCA. Deprecatory term for minor political functionaries
or officials, notaries, and "shyster" lawyers. From
the Quechua for scribe, writer, amanuensis.

QUILICO. Used to apply to hawks and falcons in general,
it was apparently derived from Quechua quillillicu,
the name for Tinnunculus cinnamomius SW.

QUINCHA. Mixture of mud and straw used in standard
"wattle" constructions of the Sierra and Costa.
Enquinchar is thus used to mean to apply plaster or
stucco.

QUINOA. Name of an Andean plant, Chenopodium quinoa,
and its seed, which latter is used as a cereal food by
the Indian population. The high protein content makes
quinoa a potentially important food source, but it has
not been successfully naturalized at lower altitudes
than about 8000 feet above sea level, nor where hu-
midity is high.

QUIPAIPAN, BATTLE OF see QUISQUIS

QUISQUIS. One of Atahualpa's most able generals. Minister of State and chief of staff of his armies. With
Calicuchima he defeated the armies of Huáscar in the
Battle of Quipaipan (1532), Atahualpa assuming domination over the Inca empire.

QUITO. Capital city of Ecuador and of the Province of

Pichincha. Population (1971 census), 551,163. Situated at an altitude of 9350 feet above the sea, and at 0º 13' south latitude, and longitude 78º 27' west of Greenwich. It lies at the foot of the now extinct or dormant volcano, Pichincha. Capital of the at least partially legendary kingdom of the Scyris, it became the seat of government and residence of the last Inca before the Spanish Conquest, Atahualpa. After Atahualpa's capture and execution by the Spaniards, Quito was destroyed by his leading general, Rumiñahui, in 1534, but upon his defeat by Benalcázar and Alvarado, it was re-established as a Spanish settlement, later that same year. After the turbulent period of the Conquest and civil wars which followed in Peru, Quito became the seat of the Real Audiencia de Quito, and residence of its president (1563). Since colonial times it has been a center of culture and art with numerous of the finest examples of Spanish Baroque architecture and plastic arts still remaining. It now is the site of two universities, and the political center of the country, but Guayaquil surpasses it in the economy.

QUITO, ACT OF. May 13, 1830--Ecuador declared independence from Gran Colombia. General Juan José Flores was elected the first president of the Republic.

QUITUS. The ancient inhabitants of the Ecuadorean area around Quito (also called Panzaleos), who gave their name to the present-day capital. See above.

- R -

RAILROADS. In 1908 the first railroad from Guayaquil to Quito was completed. A distance of 281 miles, the route from sea level to over 9000 feet or higher, it represents a real triumph in engineering. Subsequently the rails were extended northward to Ibarra, and again, to the Pacific coast at San Lorenzo, in the 1950's. From Sibambe, which lies almost due East of Guayaquil, a branch line to Cuenca was projected, but it has not been completed beyond Azogues. Other shorter lines, not a part of the main network, and constructed prior to the days of modern highways, connect the port of Caráquez with Chone; Puerto Bolívar with Piedras, Arenillas and Pasaje, as a means of bringing agricultural and other products to the coast for transport in cabotage. Since 1944 the railroads have been run by the government which took over from the English and American stockholders. Steam locomotives are gradually being replaced by diesel-powered traction, on the 727 miles of track. The rail trip from Guayaquil to Quito or vice versa is a spectacular and unforgettable experience.

RAMIREZ DAVALOS, GIL. Founder of Cuenca in 1557. A native of the city of the same name in Spain. Served temporarily as governor of Quito, and founded a number of other settlements in addition to Cuenca.

RAMIREZ DE OROZCO, JUAN. Born, 1765. Died, about 1823. Military officer and public official. General and principal aid to Presidente Goyeneche of the Audiencia of Charcas 1809-12, he led royal forces in the rebellion of Pumacagua defeating the rebels in the battle of Umachiri (March 11, 1815). President of the Audiencia of Quito, 1817-19, he was defeated along with Aymerich by Sucre in the battle of Pichincha (May 24, 1822).

RAZON, LA. Guayaquil newspaper with a circulation of 25,000. It was first issued in 1965 and has an independent editorial policy. Its director is Jorge Pérez Concha.

REAL AUDIENCIA. Primarily a judicial subdivision of the colonial government with territorial limits, which later became very important in the determination of national boundaries after independence from Spain. The audiencia of Quito was established in 1563, and was politically subject to the Viceroyalty of Peru until 1718-1740 when with the audiencias of Bogotá and Caracas it finally became part of the new Viceroyalty of Nueva Granada, and thus part of the Republic of Gran Colombia when independence was won. Subsequently the three ex-audiencias became the present-day republics of Colombia, Venezuela, and Ecuador, the latter in 1830, with the boundaries possessed by these jurisdictions in 1810. Known in jurisprudence as the doctrine of the uti possidetis of 1810, the actual boundaries so defined have still not been fixed, often as much because of a lack of definite geographical facts as to political and economic considerations. Ecuador is the nation which has doubtless suffered most because of this situation.

REGIDOR. An Indian official in the highland area appointed by the parish priest to make certain that the residents fulfill their commitments to the Church. Officials called alcaldes and alguaciles assist the regidores.

RENDON, VICTOR MANUEL. Born, December 5, 1859, Guayaquil. Died, October 9, 1940, Guayaquil. Educated in the Stanislas College and School of Medicine, Paris. Physician, diplomat and poet. Author of 29 books in Spanish and 16 in French, mostly literary in nature. Member of many learned societies.

RENDON SEMINARIO, MANUEL. Born, in 1894, Paris. Contemporary Ecuadorean painter of international renown.

REYES, OSCAR EFREN. Born in 1897, Baños. Died, December 1, 1966, Quito. Historian.

RICAURTE, ANTONIO DE. Born, June 10, 1786, Leyva, Venezuela. Died, March 25, 1814, San Mateo. Hero of the independence movement in Gran Colombia, and thus a culture hero of modern Colombia, Venezuela and Ecuador. Ricaurte was a captain under Bolívar, and in the battle between the insurgents and troops under the Spanish commander, Bóvez. When it became apparent that the arms depot which he was defending was about to fall to the enemy, Captain Ricaurte chose to remain on duty at his post after sending his men away, and to blow up the powder magazine, dying a martyr's death of sacrifice along with 300 Royalist troops. This act is within the long tradition of similar immolations by Hispanic culture heroes since Roman days.

RICKE, FRAY JODOCO. Born at Ghent, he was reputedly a close relative of Carlos V. He died at Popayán. One of the four Franciscan monks who arrived in Quito in January 1535. They opened a school, later known as the Colegio de San Andrés, to educate the children of the conquistadores and Indians.

RIOBAMBA. Capital of the Province of Chimborazo.

Population (1968 est.), 60,000.

RIOBAMBA, CONSTITUENT CONGRESS OF. On May 13,
1830, a Constituent Congress met in Riobamba to
declare the separation of Ecuador from the Union of
Gran Colombia. The Congress elected the Venezuelan
General Juan José Flores as the first President of
Ecuador. On December 11 the first Constitution of
republican Ecuador was promulgated.

RIO DE JANEIRO, PROTOCOL OF. January 29, 1942.
Also known as the Protocol of Peace, Friendship and
Boundaries, it was signed by the foreign ministers of
the contracting parties (Ecuador and Peru) and those
of the mediating powers (Argentina, Brazil, Chile,
and the United States). The protocol provided for a
new boundary line between Ecuador and Peru which
caused Ecuador to lose two-thirds of the Oriente,
which she had previously considered hers, and furthermore, deprived the nation of an outlet to the Amazon
River. On August 17, 1960, President José María
Velasco Ibarra of Ecuador declared the Protocol null
and void, and Ecuador has continued to consider it so.

RIOFRIO, JOSE LUIS see MONTUFAR Y LARREA ...

RIOFRIO, JOSE MARIA. Born, Loja. Clergyman. Deputy
from Loja Province to the 1845 Constituent Assembly;
bishop of Popeyópolis; third archbishop of Quito, 1859-
67; apostolic administrator of the Diocese of Loja.

RIOFRIO, MIGUEL. Born, Loja, 1822. Died, Peru, 1881.
Diplomat, poet, educator. Romanticist.

ROBALINO DAVILA, LUIS. Born, August 22, 1882, Quito.
Education: High School in Quito. Diplomat, historian.
Diplomatic posts in Switzerland, Mexico, Bolivia and
Brazil. Author: Orígenes del Ecuador de hoy, 1948;
Testimonio de los tiempos, 1970.

ROBLES, FRANCISCO. Born, May 5, 1811, Guayaquil.
Died, March 11, 1893, Guayaquil. Education: Naval
College. Naval officer and soldier, politician. Captain of a frigate, 1845; military commander and governor of Guayas Province, 1847; brigadier general,
1851; deputy from Manabí Province, 1852; governor of
Guayas Province, 1854-56; major general, 1876.

Presidency: elected (Constituent Convention), age 45, July 13, 1856, one term, overthrown in 1859.

ROCA, JOSE MARIA. Founded the first newspaper in Guayaquil, El Patriota Guayaquileño, August 19, 1821. Father of Roca Rodríguez (q. v.).

ROCAFUERTE, VICENTE. Born, May 1, 1783, Guayaquil. Died, May 16, 1847, Lima, Peru. Educated in Madrid in the Colegio de los Nobles, and in Paris, where he met Bolívar. Educator, writer, politician. Elected to Cortes in Spain, 1812; supreme chief of Guayaquil, 1830; supreme chief of Ecuador, October 20, 1833; deputy from Pichincha Province, 1843; president of the National Convention, 1845-46; president of the Senate, 1846; diplomat in Peru, Bolivia, Chile, 1846. Presidency: (1) non-elected (elected by a provisional assembly), age 51, 1835; (2) elected (Constituent Assembly), age 52, 1835, one term, which ended constitutionally, 1839.

ROCA RODRIGUEZ, VICENTE RAMON. Born, September 2, 1792, Guayaquil. Died, February 23, 1858, Guayaquil. Education: privately educated. Politician. Chief of police in Guayaquil, 1829; deputy at the Riobamba Convention, 1830; president of Guayaquil, 1831; vice-president of Congress, 1833; governor of Guayas Province, 1835; senator from Guayas Province, 1837-39; member of the Provisional Governing Junta, March 6, 1845 to December 7, 1845. Roca became the first president under the 1845 constitution. His father was José María Roca (q. v.). Presidency: elected (Constituent Assembly), age 53, 1845, one term, which ended constitutionally, 1849.

RODRIGUEZ DE LA PARRA Y JARAMILLO, BERNARDO. Painter, who flourished in Quito between the years 1775 and 1803, his works were largely of a religious nature contracted for by the various churches.

RODRIGUEZ DE QUIROGA, JOSE MANUAL. Born, December 8, 1771, near Cuzco, Peru. Died, August 2, 1810, Quito. Precursor of Ecuador's independence.

RODRIGUEZ LARA, GUILLERMO. Born, Nov. 16, 1923, Pujulí, Cotopaxi Province. Education: military, in Ecuador and Colombia, the U. S. Army Training School

at Fort Leavenworth, Kansas, in the United States;
engineering, in Argentina. Soldier, 33 years in the
Armed Forces. Professor in the Technical School of
Engineering, the Army War Academy, and the "Eloy
Alfaro" Military Aeronautical School. Director of
the latter. Commanding General of the Army, April,
1971. Presidency: non-elected, age 49, February 15,
1972, when a Nationalist Military Revolutionary
Government was established, forcing J. M. Velasco
Ibarra into exile.

ROJAS, ANGEL FELICISIMO. Born, December 29, 1909,
Loja. Education: J. D., University of Loja. Ecuadorean novelist and literary critic. Most important
works: Banca (novel), 1938; Un idilio bobo (novel),
1946; El éxodo de Yangana (novel), 1949.

ROLANDO, CARLOS A. Born, September 13, 1881, Guaya-
quil. Education: University of Guayaquil, 1905.
Doctor in pharmacy and chemistry. Pharmacist, bib-
liographer, historian, educator. Director of the
Municipal Chemical Laboratory in Guayaquil; member
of the Academy of History in Buenos Aires; Bolivarian
Society; Academy of History in Venezuela. Author:
Cronología del periodismo ecuatoriano, 1920; Obras
públicas ecuatorianas, 1930; Biografía del General
Juan José Flores, 1930; Crónica del periodismo en el
Ecuador, 1947.

ROMERO Y CORDERO, REMIGIO. Born, in 1896, Cuenca.
Died, August 7, 1967, Quito. A poet of high talent,
he wrote in almost every type of verse and in every
vein. Best known collections: La romería de las
carabelas, 1931; Condóricamente, 1933; his best known
individual poems: Egloga triste and Elegía de las rosas,
a sonnet.

RONDADOR. Name given to the various Ecuadorean forms of
the pan pipe employed in native musical forms.

ROSALES RAMOS, FRANCISCO. Born, December 24, 1937,
Quito. Education: J. D., Catholic University, Quito.
Lawyer, public servant, professor. Principally involved in activities relating to economic development
in Ecuador and the Andean Group, he has occupied
various posts in the Center for Development (CENDES),
and is presently president of the Institute for Foreign

Commerce and Ecuadorean Integration (ICEIE), and president of the Cartagena Accord Commission. He teaches law at both the Central University and the Catholic University in Quito, where his specialty is Industrial Legislation. He is author of La autodeterminación de los pueblos y la paz mundial.

ROYAL DECREE OF 1802 (Cédula de 1802). Issued on July 15, 1802, this decree separated from the jurisdiction of the bishop of Quito all of the region known as Mainas and Quijos, which constitutes the basin of the Marañón River within the scope of its navigable streams. The lesser tributaries and the streams above the "fall line" were not to be included. It was upon this decree, however, that the Protocol of Rio de Janeiro in 1942 was based and the boundary supposedly fixed, but Ecuador does not now recognize it.

RUBIO ORBE, GONZALO. Born, June 29, 1909, Otavalo. Education: Ph. D., Central University of Quito. Educator, historian, anthropologist. Author: Luis Felipe Borja, 1947; Nuestros indios, 1947; Eugenio de Santa Cruz y Espejo, 1950; Promociones indígenas en América, 1957; La Población Rural Ecuatoriana, 1966.

RUIZ, BARTOLOME. Ship's pilot, native of Moguer in Andalusia, who was the first Spanish explorer of the Ecuadorean coast. In 1526 he was Francisco Pizarro's chief pilot, and after leaving one of the two vessels in the expedition with his chief to explore the San Juan River, now just beyond the northern boundary of Ecuador and Colombia, he sailed southward as far as Cabo Pasado, less than half a degree below the Equator. He was thus the first European to have crossed that line in the Pacific Ocean. He met a large raft (balsa) with traders from the south, including some natives of Túmbez. He took captives, and with them, samples of the gold, silver, and textiles which they were transporting to trade along the coast. This prudent procedure rather than risking a landing enabled him to return to Pizarro with the intelligence which would bring about the conquest of the Inca empire. In 1529 he was given the title of "Grand Pilot of the Southern Ocean," and a liberal pension. Whether he actually was the first European to set foot on what is now Ecuadorean soil is open to question.

RUIZ DE CASTILLA, MANUEL URRIEZ, CONDE DE. Died,
Quito, 1812. Military officer, public official. Chief
magistrate of Chillques and Masques (Paruro), 1780.
Fought against the rebels in the Túpac Amarú uprising
and stayed in Cuzco with the Royal forces, 1783.
Ruíz de Castilla obtained the title of conde, 1790;
president of the Audiencia of Quito, August 1, 1808-
11. Captured by the 1809 revolutionary junta and confined, he persecuted its members when the royal
government was re-established, but was forced out of
the government once more and "died shortly afterward, an unhappy death."

RUIZ DE SANTO DOMINGO Y GARCIA, JUAN. Born,
Panama, 173?, died, 178?, Guayaquil. J.D. (civil
and canon law), Real Universidad, Quito. Lawyer and
public servant, judge.

RUMAZO GONZALEZ, ALFONSO. Born, March 12, 1908,
Latacunga. Education: Secondary Schooling. Historian,
biographer, diplomat. Author: Gobernantes del Ecuador, 1932; El congreso de 1933, 1934; Manuela Sáenz,
la libertadora del libertador, 1944; Simón Bolívar,
1950; and Sucre, gran Mariscal de Ayacucho, 1963.

RUMIÑAHUI [Face of Stone]. Born, 1446. Died, 1535.
Probably the most brilliant of Atahualpa's generals
who helped him defeat the forces of his half brother,
Huáscar. He continued the fight against the Spaniards
and was defeated by Sebastián de Benalcázar after a
long and bitter struggle. Rumiñahui was captured and
executed in 1535.

- S -

SAAD, PEDRO ANTONIO. Born, 1909, Guayaquil. Education: J.D., University of Guayaquil. Politician,
businessman. Founder and secretary general of the
Communist-oriented Confederation of Ecuadorean
Workers (CTE), 1944; member, Constituent Assembly,
1944-45; secretary general of the Communist Party
of Ecuador (PCE); functional Senator for labor representing the Coast; organizer of the Communist-oriented
Popular Democratic Union (UDP), 1968.

SACOTO ARIAS, AUGUSTO. Born, 1907, Azogues, Cañar
Province. Poet, dramatist, lawyer, diplomat. Editor of the literary magazine, Mar Pacífico.

SAENZ, JOSE MARIA. Born, Quito, between 1795 and 1800.
Died, near Tabacundo, April 20, 1834. Military man.
He first served in the Spanish army, but as soon as
the war for independence began, he and others in his
battalion, "Infante," joined the insurgency. He fought
with distinction in Colombia, attaining the rank of
general, and then proceeded to Quito, where he participated in the Battle of Pichincha, which freed Ecuador. He opposed the separatist movement of General
Flores. He was finally cornered near the Hacienda
of Pisillo not far from Tabacundo, forced to surrender,
and then murdered.

SAENZ, MANUELA. Born, December 1793, Quito. Died,
November 23, 1856, Paita, Peru. Heroine of the independence movement, who left her husband, Jaime
Thorne, a wealthy English merchant, to join Bolívar
after his arrival in Quito in 1822. On September 25,
1828, she saved his life when he was attacked by
assassins in Bogotá, Colombia. She died in exile in
Peru. She was called "La Libertadora del Libertador"
(The Liberator of the Liberator), and held the rank
of colonel in the army of Gran Colombia.

SALAS. Family name of a long line of Ecuadorean artists:
Antonio Salas, born before 1790 at Quito; died, 1860.
Painter of note and ability. Works in the cathedral
Museum of Art and elsewhere in Quito. He painted
portraits of Bolívar, Sucre, and other officers of the
independence movement from life. Ramón Salas, elder
son of Antonio and father of Camilo (died 1905), and
Alejandro Salas, also artists. Sons of Alejandro were
Carlos, Manuel, and José Salas--the latter was an
artist who died in Rome while holding a scholarship
from the Ecuadorean government. Rafael Salas was
the second son of Antonio. He became an able landscapist, studied at Rome under a government scholarship, returned to the Academy of Fine Arts established
by García Moreno, received a life pension from the
government and died at Quito, March 24, 1906.

SALASACA. A dispersed Indian community of about 5000
subsistence farmers, located about nine miles southeast

of Ambato in Tungurahua Province. The Salasaca
Indians have successfully fought off encroachment by
non-Indians and have remained aggressively defensive
against outsiders. Although their origin is uncertain,
one speculation is that they may have been transplanted
from Bolivia by the Incas.

SALAZAR, VICENTE LUCIO. Born, December 20, 1832,
Quito. Died, February 14, 1896, Quito. Education:
J. D. Lawyer, politician. Secretary of Ecuadorean
Legation in Colombia, deputy from Pichincha Province
and president of that Chamber, 1896; minister of the
Treasury, 1883; president of the Senate, 1892; vice-
president of the republic, 1895. Presidency: non-
elected, age 62, 1895, when he took over from the
incumbent, Luis Cordero Crespo, who was forced to
resign.

SALAZAR ALVEAR, FRANCISCO JAVIER. Born, 1739?,
Quito. Died, 1802?, Quito. Education: J. D., University of Santo Tomás, Quito. Lawyer. Served as
attorney for the presidency of the Audiencia, under
Diguja, Muñoz de Guzmán, Villalengua, and Carondelet. He was a member of the Revolutionary Senate
of 1809 and executor of the estates of some of the con-
spirators who were murdered for which reason he was
later barred from the practice of law. Father of various leaders of the independence movement, among his
sons were Agustín and Joaquín Salazar y Lozano.

SALAZAR ARBOLEDA, FRANCISCO JAVIER. Born, Quito,
1824. Died, Guayaquil, September 21, 1891. Educated
in Ecuador and Germany. Lawyer. General of the
republic (army), minister of the Interior and Foreign
Affairs, and of War and Navy; state governor, president of the Convention of 1884. Diplomat, linguist,
legislator, juris-consult, educator, orator, poet.
Member of several American and European learned
societies. Author of various texts for public schools
and the Army.

SALAZAR Y LOZANO, AGUSTIN. Born ca. 1782, Quito;
died 1862. J. D. Seminary College of San Luis. He
served as judge of superior and supreme courts.
Taught at the University in Quito, to the faculty of
which he was appointed by Rocafuerte. Historian of
the early republic.

SALGÜERO, ANTONIO. Born 1864, son of Josefina Salas,
a daughter of Antonio Salas. Painter who learned his
art in the studio of his cousin, Alejandro Salas.
Studied at Rome. Professor of art at the School of
Fine Arts in Quito. Religious subjects and folklore
were his chief interests. His works are in the Colegio
de La Dolorosa and in the Cotocallo Museum in
Quito.

SALINAS. Port and ocean resort 95 miles from Guayaquil
on Santa Elena Peninsula. Sport fishing and fine
beaches are its attractions. A hot sulphur spring
and spa are close by at San Vicente.

SALINAS LOYOLA, JUAN DE. Spanish captain, explorer
who discovered principal tributaries of the Amazon
River on his expedition from Loja, 1557-59, during
which he explored the Santiago and the Ucayali rivers.
Appointed governor of Yaguarzongo and Bracamoros
Province in 1566.

SALINAS ZENITAGOYA, JUAN JOSE. Born, November 24,
1755, Sangolquí. Died, August 2, 1810, Quito. Criollo
officer in Spanish army. When he and other native-
born members of the armed forces failed to receive
promotions (because of their New World origins), they
went over to the independence movement. Salinas was
made a colonel at the head of a large force, but
Spanish superiority in arms and men brought defeat.
Salinas was captured and murdered in jail in Quito.

SALOMON-LOZANO TREATY. March 24, 1922. Treaty
signed in secret at Lima whereby Colombia ceded to
Peru territory previously ceded her by Ecuador. When
the Ecuador government became aware of the agreement October 31, 1925, she severed diplomatic relations with Colombia.

SALVADOR, HUMBERTO. Born, December 25, 1909,
Guayaquil. Education: J.D., Central University of
Quito. Ecuadorean novelist and professor. His
writings are concerned with the city dweller. Major
works: Ajedrez (short stories), 1929; En la ciudad
he perdido una novela (novel), 1930; Taza de té (short
stories), 1932; Camarada (novel), 1933; Trabajadores
(novel), 1935; Noviembre (novel), 1939; La novela
interrumpida (novel), 1942; Prometeo (novel), 1943;

Universidad Central, 1944; La fuente clara (novel),
1946.

SAMANIEGO Y JARAMILLO, MANUEL. Born, about 1767,
Quito. Died, 1824. The most famous Ecuadorean
painter of the 18th century. Known for his landscapes,
he also wrote a treatise on painting. Considered as
his best works are: "The Birth of the Christchild"
and the "Assumption of the Virgin Mary."

SAN CRISTOBAL. Capital of the Galápagos Islands. Located on the island of San Cristóbal (English: Chatham
Island).

SAN ILDEFONSO, TREATY OF see AMAZON RIVER

SAN LORENZO. Northernmost Ecuadorean seaport. Con-
nected to Quito by rail.

SANCHEZ DE ORELLANA, FERNANDO FELIX. Born,
Latacunga, 1716. Educated in the Colegio de San
Luis and San Fernando, Quito. Public official.
Lieutenant governor of Quito; President of the Audi-
encia of Quito, March 10, 1745 to September 21,
1753.

SANGAY. An active volcano in the Eastern Cordillera.
Elevation 17,159 feet.

SANJUANITO. Popular lively musical form, called huayno
in Peru, and danced indiscriminately by both men
and women. The music is often played by a group of
rondadores and quenas.

SANTA ELENA PENINSULA. The farthest point west on
the Ecuadorean coastline above Guayaquil, and the area
of the first oilfields in the country, now almost ex-
hausted.

SANTACRUZ Y ESPEJO, FRANCISCO EUGENIO DE. Born,
February 21, 1747, Quito. Died, December 27, 1795,
Quito. M.D. Quito. 1767. Physician, journalist,
literary critic. Founder of the National Library and
the first Ecuadorean journal, Las Primicias de la
Cultura de Quito, 1792. One of the most important
men of letters during the colonial period, he suffered
imprisonment for his liberal views.

SANTANDER, FRANCISCO DE PAULA. Born, April 13, 1792, Cúcuta, Colombia. Died, May 6, 1840, Bogotá. Military leader and statesman. Doctor of Laws, 1809, Santo Rosario de Cúcuta. He fought in the Wars for Independence, beginning in 1810, and afterwards served as governor of the department (state) of Cudinamarca. He participated in the Battle of Pichincha which established the independence of the area which was to become Ecuador. Elected president of Colombia in 1832, he served in that capacity until 1837.

SANTIAGO, MIGUEL DE. Born, 1625, Alto Buenos Aires, Santiago Parish, Quito. Died, January 4, 1706, Quito. Probably the most famous Ecuadorean painter of the 17th century, whose works were admired as far away as Rome. His best works can be seen in the Convent of San Agustín in Quito. The son of Lucas Viznate and Juana Ruiz, he took the name Miguel de Santiago when adopted by Don Hernando de Santiago. He was a teacher of Nicolás Javier de Goríbar.

SANTIAGO DE GUAYAQUIL. Full, original name of Guayaquil, so named because of its founding on St. James's day, July 25, 1537, by Francisco de Orellana.

SANTIAGO RIVER. A tributary of the Marañón River, it rises in the eastern Ecuadorean Andes in the province of Santiago Morona and flows almost due south into the mainstream, which is itself the principal southern tributary of the Amazon.

SANTIANA, ANTONIO. Born, 1914, Quito. Anthropologist. Professor at the Central University in Quito, author of numerous studies in anthropology and folklore, and organizer of a number of national and international conferences.

SANTILLAN, FERNANDO DE. Died, 1575. Public official and chronicler. Santillán arrived in Peru in 1548 to serve as magistrate of Lima. By decree of Philip II, September 21, 1563, he became the first president of the Audiencia of Quito as of September 18, 1564. Appointed bishop of Charcas (Bolivia), in 1572, he died before he could reach there. Founder of the Royal Hospital at Quito, and author of Historia de los Incas y relaciones de mi gobierno, 1563.

SAPUYES.   Site of the battle disastrous to the insurgents,
October 16, 1809.

SARAGURO.   Indian group numbering about 10,000 living
in the southernmost province of Loja.   Possibly
descendents of a cañari group, or transplants brought
into the region by the Incas from Bolivia, the group
is progressive, principally agricultural, largely land-
owning and prosperous.

SARAGURO.   Site of the battle in southern Loja in which
Sucre as leader of the forces supporting New Granada
(present day Venezuela, Colombia, and Ecuador) against
Lamar, who sought to extend Peruvian holdings to include at least southern Ecuador.   Sucre was victorious February 12, 1829.

SARAMULLO.   In the Spanish of the costa the word is used
to describe a playful, mischievous or undisciplined
child.

SCHOOLS.   There are two school systems in Ecuador to
all intents and purposes: the public and the private.
Public schools are in the great majority elementary,
and provide educational opportunities for somewhat
under one million pupils, with the greatest concentration in the larger cities and provincial capitals.   Secondary schools are few in number and almost entirely
restricted to the larger cities.   There are about
20,000 elementary school teachers in the government
schools which provide six years of instruction in the
cities, but are restricted to four years in most rural
areas.   There are perhaps 10,000 secondary teachers.
Secondary schooling is for six years and is provided
in three types of institutions: academic, vocational,
and pre-normal.   Graduates of the academic colegios,
as they are called, are possible candidates for the
university and receive the bachillerato.   Others are
not eligible for the university.
     Privately owned and operated schools are largely
run by the Roman Catholic Church, but there are also
non-sectarian schools in Guayaquil and Quito, operated
as a means to a livelihood by their owners.   All are
registered with the Ministry of Education, but are
loosely supervised.   Middle and upper class families
have no great confidence in the government schools and
send their children, often at a sacrifice, to the privately
operated institutions.

Since the resources for operation of the school
system are inadequate and the rural families, especially, cannot afford to send their children to school
for six years, the great mass of the population is
limited to no more than three years of schooling.
Further, because the population growth is greater than
the ability to provide classrooms and teachers, the
present illiteracy is about 40 per cent, a reduction
from the 60 per cent of 30 years ago, but still high.

SCHWARZ, JUAN ADAN, S. J.   German Jesuit in charge
of the first printing press in Ecuador.   The press
was brought to Ecuador by the Jesuits in 1755 and in-
stalled in Ambato.

SCYRI.   Title used by the rulers of the so-called "Kingdom of the Quitus," conquered by the Inca Huayna
Cápac, 1460-1485.

SEADTA   see   SOCIEDAD ECUATORIANA DE TRANSPORTES

SECOYA.   An Indian tribe living in the northernmost part
of Ecuador's Oriente near the Putumayo River.   The
Secoyas number about 600 and have not been hostile
to Europeans.   With the discovery of oil in the region,
their survival is in doubt, as always when Europeans
and mestizos enter a primitive area.

SECRETARIO.   Office manager of the political delegate,
charged with maintenance of civil records, etc.

SELVA ALEGRE, MARQUES DE   see   MONTUFAR Y
FRASSO ... and   MONTUFAR Y LARREA ...

SENIERGUES, JUAN [Jean Siniergues].   Born, France.
Died, August 29, 1739, Cuenca.   French medical man
who accompanied the La Condamine Expedition to
Ecuador.   While the surveys were in progress in the
neighborhood of Cuenca, Seniergues lent medical aid
to a number of persons in the community.   Whether
it was because of professional jealousies or religious
prejudices it has long been not clear, but a mob
gathered on the night of August 28, things got out of
hand, and Seniergues was severely injured and died
the next day.   The matter became somewhat of a cause
célèbre which for two centuries remained a blot on the
history of the community because of a letter of La

Condamine to his wife in which he sought to exonerate
the Frenchman on the basis of local superstitions and
prejudices against foreigners.   Octavio Cordero Palacios
in the 1920's re-studied the matter exhaustively, leaving little doubt that certain amorous escapades of the
dead medical man were behind the sentiments against
him.

SERRANO.   A person living in or native to the highland
   (sierra).

SHUNGO.   Sweetheart, "honey-bunch," or "sweetie."   Often
   heard in popular parlance and songs.

SIERRA.   Andean highland which includes the two parallel
   cordilleras of the Andean chain which cut through
   Ecuador.   The Sierra covers approximately 27, 500
   square miles, about one-fourth of Ecuador's national
   territory.   Politically, the Sierra is divided into ten
   provinces: Azuay, Bolívar, Cañar, Carchi, Chimborazo, Cotopaxi, Imbabura, Loja, Pichincha, and
   Tungurahua.

SILVA, MEDGARDO ANGEL.   Born 1899, Guayaquil; died,
   suicide, 1919.   Poet.   With Humberto Fierro, Ernesto
   Noboa Caamaño, and Arturo Borja he formed the
   first group of Ecuadorean post-modernist poets.   His
   scant economic resources contrasted with the exoti-
   cism of his poet's imagination led to his suicide.

SIVEWRIGHT, SIR JAMES.   Born, 1848, Fochaber, Scotland.
   Died, September 10, 1916 in a Shropshire nursing
   home.   Scotch financier and British public official
   who underwrote loans for the Guayaquil-Quito railroad.

SOCIALISMO UNIFICADO.   A splinter group of the Partido
   Socialista Ecuatoriano (q. v.) headed by Carlos Cueva
   Tamariz.   Founded in 1966, elected one deputy and
   one senator to the nation's Congress in 1968.   The
   movement is primarily based in the Sierra.

SOCIEDAD DE CACAHUEROS.   A labor group composed of
   the urban cacao workers.   It was one of the first
   labor groups to organize in Ecuador (1908).   Ideo-
   logically it was influenced by Bakunin's anarchism.

SOCIEDAD ECUATORIANA DE TRANSPORTES (SEADTA).
A German-Ecuadorean airline company organized in
1937. The airline, which never had more than three
planes in simultaneous service, operated approximately
900 route miles and served the cities of Quito, Guayaquil, Cuenca, Loja, Esmeraldas, Manta, and Salinas.
This service was terminated in late 1941 when the
airline was unable to acquire fuel for its planes.

SOLANO, FRAY VICENTE DOMINGO. Born, October 16,
1791, Cuenca. Died, April 2, 1865, Cuenca. Clergyman. Franciscan monk who was widely known for his
scientific exploits; wrote numerous books and pamphlets
covering such diverse fields as theology and botany.
His Obras completas was published in Barcelona, 1892-
95.

SOSOYA, JUAN. Born, Navarre. Clergyman, public offi-
cial. Chief magistrate in Guatemala; president of the
Audiencia of Quito 1707-14; knight of the Order of
Santiago.

STEVENSON, WILLIAM BENNETT. Born in England about
1787. Died sometime after 1825, in England. British
traveler who occupied several important posts in Ecua-
dor--e.g., secretary to the captain general of Quito,
governor of Esmeraldas, and also secretary to Lord
Cochrane. He was author of the three-volume Historical and Descriptive Narrative of Twenty Years
Residence in South America, 1825, in which he partly
describes his experiences in Ecuador.

SUAREZ RODRIGUEZ, ANTONIO. Dean of the judges of
the Audiencia of Quito, who acted as president of the
Audiencia from the death of the Baron de Carondelet, until the arrival of the Conde Ruiz de Castilla,
1807-08.

SUAREZ VEINTIMILLA, MARIANO. Born, June 6, 1897,
Ibarra. Education: law, Central University of Quito.
Lawyer, politician. Several times deputy from
Pichincha Province to nation's Congress; vice-president
of that Chamber; president of the National Convention,
1946-47; minister of Agriculture and of the Treasury;
vice-president of the republic (under José María
Velasco Ibarra) 1946-47, succeeded to the presidency,
non-elected, September 2, 1947-September 19, 1947.

Head of the Conservative Party on several occasions.

SUCO.   Red-headed.

SUCRE.   The national monetary unit fixed at 49.3706 milli-
grams of fine gold and containing 100 centavos.   There
is presently an official rate and a fluctuating free
market rate.   As of September 1972, the official buy-
ing rate was S/-24.75 and the selling rate was S/-25.25.
The fluctuating free market rate was S/-27.30.   The one
sucre coin is popularly called un ayora after President
Isidro Ayora, (1926-31), in whose time it was first
coined.   The sucre is cupro-nickel at present, but
originally was minted as a silver coin of the same size
as the dollar as well as in gold of various denomina-
tions; abbreviation: S/- .   Named for Antonio José de
Sucre.

SUCRE, ANTONIO JOSE DE.   Born, February 3, 1795,
Cumaná, Venezuela.   Died, June 4, 1830, Berruecos,
Colombia.   Military, politician.   Public service:
fought in the wars of independence; defeated the Peruvians in the battle of Portete de Tarqui, February 27,
1829.   An Ecuadorean national hero.   When word
reached Simón Bolívar of his assassination in 1830, he
exclaimed: "They have slain Abel. "

SWETT PALOMEQUE, JORGE ENRIQUE.   Born, 1925,
Guayaquil.   Educated at the Colegio Vicente Rocafuerte
in Guayaquil and in the law school of the University.
Professor, painter and muralist.   Student of archeology.
Swett has traveled and exhibited abroad, but his murals,
totaling over 40, are his principle work.   They appear
in the Guayaquil airport and the marine port building,
public library, and city hall in Guayaquil.

- T -

TABARA, ENRIQUE.   Born in 1930, Guayaquil.   Educated
at the School of Fine Arts, Guayaquil.   Contemporary
Ecuadorean painter.

TAGUA.   A palm nut (vegetable ivory), fruit of Phytelephas
macrocarpa, which is abundant in the coastal provinces
of Esmeraldas and Manabí.   It is dried and exported

primarily for the making of buttons. Locally it is used
for making carved jewelry, toys and dice.

TAITA.   "Father. "   Often used by the indigenous population
when referring to their superiors.

TAMAYO, JOSE LUIS.   Born, July 29, 1858, Chanduy
(Guayas Province).   Died, July 7, 1947, Guayaquil.
Education: J. D., 1886. Lawyer, politician.   Civil
and military chief of Manabí Province, 1895; under-
secretary of Foreign Relations; minister of Interior;
president of the Chamber of Deputies, 1898-99; senator from Esmeraldas Province, 1902-1905.   Presidency: elected (popular), age 62, 1920, one term,
which ended constitutionally in 1924.

TAMBO.   Historic word designating the points of stopover
or relay on the Incan highway system, and later as
the designation of inns and eating houses on stagecoach
routes.

TARQUI.   River and site of the battle, February 26-27, 1829,
between the forces of Gran Colombia and Peru, in which
the Peruvians were defeated and on the following day
signed the Treaty of Girón recognizing the separation
of the two areas with the boundaries of pre-independence New Granada and Peru.   Tarqui, in the province
of Azuay, near the city of Cuenca, was also the southern triangulation point of La Condamine Equatorial
survey.

TEJAR.   An archeological zone in the Guayas basin which
dates back to 200 B. C.   The Tejar phase shares with
the Daule phase location and date of origin.   The pottery of both phases share with Jambelí zone the painted
decoration while the shapes appear similar to those of
the Guangala phase.

EL TELEGRAFO.   Oldest newspaper in Ecuador, founded in
Guayaquil on February 16, 1884.   Its daily circulation
is 25, 000.   It has an independent editorial policy and
is directed by Dr. Abel Romeo Castillo Castillo.

TENA.   Capital of Napo Province.   Population (1968 est.),
less than 10, 000.

TENA.   Settlement founded by Gil Ramírez Dávalos (q. v.)

in 1560 on the eastern slopes of the Andes.

TENIENTE POLITICO. Political deputy, appointed civil officer, often also the representative of the hacendado.

TENTH OF AUGUST. Ecuadorean national independence day, celebrated on this date because in 1809 a group composed of Juan Pío Montúfar, Marqués of Selva Alegre, President; Bishop Juan Larrea; Manuel Rodríguez de Quiroga; Dr. Antonio Ante; and others, met at home of Manuela Cañizares in Quito and formed a Supreme Governmental Junta, drew up a Declaration of Independence, the first in Spanish America, and were able to maintain their organization until October 23 of that year, when it was suppressed by Royal authority.

TETETE. A small, little-known Indian tribe which inhabits the jungle region on the Colombian and Ecuadorean side of the Putumayo river close to the 76th parallel. Only three men of the tribe, which may number around 250 to 300 members, have been in contact with the outside world. So far, they have refused to reveal the location of their villages.

TIAONE. An archeological zone on the Ecuadorean coast between Cape San Francisco and the mouth of the Río Esmeraldas. It dates back between 500 B. C. and A. D. 500. Little is known of this zone except that it displays distinct pottery characteristics and that figurines are less common.

EL TIEMPO. Newspaper published in Quito with a daily circulation of 10, 000. It was first published in November 1, 1964, and has a conservative editorial policy. Its director is Dr. Carlos de la Torre Reyes.

TOBAR, CARLOS R. Born, Quito, 1854, died, Barcelona, May 12, 1920. M. D. , Central University of Quito. Physician, scientist, educator. Tobar taught literature in the Central University, became the dean of the School of Letters, and rector of the same. Vicepresident of the Senate in 1900, he occupied various ministries. In 1912 with the fall of the Alfaro government he chose self-exile and died in Spain.

TOBAR DONOSO, JULIO. Born, January 25, 1894. Education: J. D. , Central University of Quito, 1917.

Diplomat, lawyer, historian. Minister of Foreign
Relations, 1941-42; imprisoned July 22, 1944 because
of his part in negotiation of the 1942 Protocol of Río
de Janeiro; minister of the Supreme Court, 1957-69.
Author: Monografías históricas, 1937; La invasión
peruana y el Protocolo de Río, 1945.

TOBAR-RIO BRANCO TREATY. May 6, 1904. Ecuador
ceded some 120,000 square kilometers to Brazil and
the boundary between the two nations was recognized:
i. e., Brazil specifically took cognizance of Ecuador
as a nation with which it had a common boundary.
Under the 1942 Protocol of Río de Janeiro this is no
longer the case.

TOLA. A word used to designate any of several pre-
Columbian burial places found by the conquistadors and
rifled for their valuables.

TOLITA. An archeological zone in the mouth of the Río
Santiago on the far northern coast of Esmeraldas
Province. The zone is estimated to date between
500 B. C. and A. D. 500. It is rich in figurines and
other ceramic pieces, as well as gold objects.

TORRE REYES, CARLOS DE LA. Born, December 23,
1928, Quito. Education: J. D. , Catholic University of
Ecuador, Quito, 1954. Lawyer, journalist, diplomat,
historian. Editor-in-chief, El Tiempo, Quito, since its
inception in 1965. His legal career has been concerned
with banking and the administration of banking law, with
the administration of the agrarian reform under the
Institute for Agrarian Reform and Colonization.

TOTORA. Reed, cattail. The Ecuadorean variety, Scyrpus
totora, is much used by native artisans, especially for
the weaving of mats. The same was and is used to
make boats.

TRIBUNAL DE GARANTIAS CONSTUTUCIONALES. The
Court of Constitutional Guarantees is an autonomous
institution with national jurisdiction. Its duties are
primarily: 1) to see to it that the constitution is
faithfully applied; 2) to hear complaints pertaining to
the violation of the constitution; and 3) to formulate
observations concerning decrees, rules, and regula-
tions issued in violation of the constitution. The

Tribunal has ten members.

TRIBUNAL SUPREMO ELECTORAL (TSE). The Supreme
Electoral Tribunal is an autonomous agency created by
the 1945 Constitution and established in 1947. The
TSE is in charge of conducting and supervising elections. Only the TSE can proclaim the official election
results. The electoral machinery, at the lowest level
is composed of a polling place (mesa). The polling
places in each province are supervised by each provincial electoral tribunal, which in turn, is responsible
to the Supreme Electoral Tribunal.

TRIBUNALES DE CONTENCIOSOS. The Redress and Public
Claims Courts are autonomous institutions which function independently from other tribunals and have national
jurisdiction. The administrative court reviews resolu-
tions of public and semi-public agencies. Fiscal
tribunals hear tax cases.

TRISTE. A popular music form, sung in a melancholy tone,
to the accompaniment of a native flute-like instrument
or fife (pífano), guitar and harp. It is apparently of
indigenous origin and common only to the Sierra, not
the Costa.

TROYA IBARRA, RAFAEL. Born, October 25, 1845,
Ibarra. Died, March 10, 1921, Ibarra. Painter.
An excellent landscapist and student of the flora of
his native country. His works reside in the cathedral
collections at Ibarra, and in the church at Atuntaqui,
as well as in private collections.

TSANTSAS. The name given by the Jívaro Indians to the
human heads shrunken and dried and used in some of
their rituals.

TSE see TRIBUNAL SUPREMO ELECTORAL

TULCAN. Capital city of Carchi Province located on the
Pan American Highway at the Colombian border. Tulcán is at an altitude of 9000 feet and its population
(1968 est.) is 20,000.

TUMBEZ. An Indian tribe which inhabited the southern coast
of Ecuador. They were absorbed relatively early by
the Inca empire and were difficult to distinguish as a

tribal entity at the time of the Spanish conquest.

TUMBEZ [also, Tumbes]. The present-day city, now in
    Peru, is close to the spot where the conquistadors
    under Francisco Pizarro first entered the mainland
    of South America. It was an important Inca city, and,
    when seen from the sea before an invasion was at-
    tempted, urged the Spaniards to greater efforts.

TUNCAHUAN. An archeological zone located in the Rio-
    bamba basin. Estimates of the age of the zone vary
    between 500 B. C. and A. D. 500.

TUNGURAHUA. Province in the central Ecuadorean high-
    lands. Area 1366 square miles; population (1968 est.),
    247, 000. So called for the volcano of the same name,
    16, 690 feet in altitude.

TUPAC-YUPANQUI. An Inca emperor who began his cam-
    paign by conquering present-day Ecuador in 1455, and
    after a long struggle succeeded in conquering the
    southern provinces in the early 1470's.

                        - U -

UCAYALI RIVER. A stream arising in the eastern moun-
    tainous region of Peru and joining the Marañón some
    distance above Iquitos. Its discovery by Juan de
    Salinas Loyola in the expedition from Loja, 1557-59,
    was one of the allegations of jurisdiction by right of
    discovery advanced by the Ecuadoreans in boundary
    disputes with Peru.

UDNA see UNION DEMOCRATICA NACIONAL ANTI-
    CONSERVADORA

UDP see UNION DEMOCRATICA POPULAR

UHLE, MAX. Born, March 25, 1871, Dresden, Saxony.
    Died, May 11, 1944, Loben, Upper Silesia. German
    archeologist, father of Peruvian and Ecuadorean
    archeology. His work in Ecuador, 1919-33, included
    discovery of the remains of the palace of Huayna-
    Cápac at Coshisqui, on which his popular fame rests,
    although his systematization of the archeological

remains of the Andean region has never been super-
seded.

ULLOA, ANTONIO. Born, in 1716. Died in 1795. Spanish
    scientist, member of the La Condamine Expedition (q. v.),
    liberal critic of the colonial Spanish regime, and gov-
    ernor of Louisiana, 1766-68.

ULTIMAS NOTICIAS. The evening edition of El Comercio,
    founded on June 8, 1938. It has a daily circulation of
    30, 000.

UNION DEMOCRATICA NACIONAL ANTI-CONSERVADORA
    (UDNA). A leftist ad-hoc coalition which was formed
    during the 1960 presidential campaign in support of
    Dr. Antonio Parra Velasco (president) and Dr. Manuel
    Benjamín Carrión (vice-president). The coalition was
    supported by the CFP, PSRE, PCE, and URJE. It
    crystallized out of the so-called "Second Independence
    Movement"--i. e., economic independence, as a con-
    tinuation of the unfinished work of the "First Indepen-
    dence" from Spain and that initiated by General Eloy
    Alfaro in 1895, both of which were political in nature.
    Its motto was "Bread, Culture and Liberty. " The
    UDNA ticket finished last in 1960 with 6 per cent of
    the valid votes cast.

UNION DEMOCRATICA POPULAR (UDP). A coalition move-
    ment formed by Communist elements prior to the 1968
    presidential election. The movement supported the
    candidacies of Elías Gallegos Anda (president) and
    Gonzalo Villalba (vice-president). Both finished in
    last place with less than 2 per cent of the valid vote.

UNION NACIONAL DE PERIODISTAS (UNP). National
    Union of Journalists.

UNION REVOLUCIONARIA DE LA JUVENTUD ECUATORIANA
    (URJE). A pro-Castro organization of militant high
    school and university students which was organized out
    of a movement initially called "Second Independence"
    and supported the unsuccessful left-wing Parra-Carrión
    ticket in the 1960 presidential election. URJE was
    quite successful in the days of President Carlos Julio
    Arosemena Monroy (1961-63), especially in Guayaquil.
    The movement is of no importance today.

UNIVERSITIES.   Various institutions of university level
were early established at Quito, for example: the
Colegio de San Andrés, created by the Franciscan
order in about 1555, continuing until 1581.   Because
of conflicts of interest and policy, various others
were established and closed, until 1596, when a papal
decree authorized the Colegio de San Nicolás Tolentino,
to be operated by the Augustinians.   Most prestigious
of the colonial universities was that of St. Thomas
Aquinas, which began operations under a Royal decree
on April 9, 1688.   The Jesuits had operated the University of St. Gregory the Great from 1622, under a
papal bull; and the Dominicans, the College of St.
Ferdinand, from 1681.   All were consolidated into the
University of Quito in 1776.   After independence, on
January 1, 1826, the Central University of Quito took
over in its place.   There are now 17 institutions of
higher learning in Ecuador: Cuenca (1868), Guayaquil
(1867), Loja, and Manabí, in addition to Quito, are
national.   There are Catholic universities in Guayaquil
and Quito, and the National Polytechnic Institute of
Quito, established in 1870, as well as several normal
schools.

EL UNIVERSO.   Largest daily newspaper in Ecuador with
a daily circulation of about 90, 000.   It was first published in Guayaquil on September 16, 1921.   It has an
independent editorial policy and is directed by the
Pérez Castro family.

UNP   see   UNION NACIONAL DE PERIODISTAS

URBINA VITERI, JOSE MARIA.   Born (baptised), May 13,
1808, Quito.   Died, September 4, 1891, Guayaquil.
Education: Naval Academy of Guayaquil.   Soldier,
politician.   Colonel, 1835; deputy from Loja Province,
1843; governor of Manabí Province, 1845; deputy from
Pichincha Province; president of the Chamber of
Deputies, 1849; civil and military chief of Guayaquil,
1850; deputy from Guayas Province, 1850; deputy from
Guayas Province to 1878 Constituent Convention; minister to Chile, 1879; chief of staff, 1880.   Presidency:
(1)   non-elected, age 43, 1851 (overthrew President
Diego Noboa) to 1852; (2)   elected (Constituent Convention) age 44, 1852, one term, which ended constitutionally, 1856.   Remembered for his freeing of Ecuador's negro slaves, 1852.

URDANETA, LUIS. Born, Coro, Venezuela. Died, July
30, 1831, Panama. Criollo officer in the Spanish
forces who went over to the patriot movement. Successful in many battles against the Spaniards, he
later was defeated and captured by the Royalists.
Freed when the 1822 constitutional group was restored
in Spain, he became a general under Bolívar. Urdaneta
opposed Ecuadorean union with Gran Colombia, went to
Panama, where he took part in an uprising, was captured, court-martialed and shot.

URJE see UNION REVOLUCIONARIA . . .

URRIEZ, MANUEL see RUIZ DE CASTILLA . . .

UZCATEQUI, EMILIO. Born, May 11, 1899, Quito. Education: J. D., Central University of Quito. Educator,
historian. Functional senator for Education, 1930-35;
deputy from Pichincha Province, 1944-45; dean of
Faculty of Philosophy, Central University, 1949-55;
head of UNESCO missions to Paraguay, 1955-59, El
Salvador, 1959-60, and Bolivia, 1961-64. Author:
Historia del Ecuador, 2 Vols., 1955.

- V -

VACAS GALINDO, PEDRO ENRIQUE. Born, April 1, 1865,
Cotacachi, Imbabura. Died, June 11, 1938, Quito.
Historian, novelist, internationalist. Counselor in
the Ecuadorean Embassy in Washington, he wrote a
three-volume work on the Ecuadorean-Peruvian boundary
question (1902-1903), and a novel, Nankijukima, with
the customs and mores of the Jívaro Indians (1894).
His geographic-historical map of Ecuador (1906) was
for a long time used in Ecuador's high schools and
universities.

VALDEZ, ENRIQUE. Born, in 1868. Died, April 11, 1914.
Plantation owner who participated in uprising against
conservative President Luis Cordero, 1895, he became a military leader, supporting Eloy Alfaro. Later
he led troops against Alfaro (1912), and helped overthrow him. He was killed April 11, 1914, in a fight
with Negro insurrectionists.

VALDIVIA. The oldest archeological ceramic type yet to be

reported in the Western Hemisphere. The period is
named after a fishing village on the northern Guayas
coast and dates back to 3200 B. C. and lasted some
2000 years. The most prominent examples of this
phase are pottery figurines with a recessed flat face,
long neck and carefully executed coiffure.

VALVERDE, MIGUEL. Born, December 6, 1852, Guayaquil.
Died, 1920, at Rome, Italy. Pamphleteer, newspaperman, diplomat, country school teacher. One of the
principal opponents of García Moreno and Veintimilla,
and founder with Federico Proaño of the newspaper,
La Nueva Era, in Guayaquil.

VALVERDE, VICENTE DE. Born, Oropesa (Toledo), Spain.
Murdered by Indians in Peru in November, 1542.
Dominican priest with Pizarro who, tradition says,
unswervingly condemned the Inca Atahualpa and his
court as idolaters, but insisted upon "conversion" to
Christianity before their execution by the Spaniards.
Later historians have agreed that Valverde, like his
fellow Dominican, Bartolomé de las Casas, was a
leader in the defense of the native population, and,
in spite of his part in the Conquest, a humanitarian.

VALVERDE-CORNEJO PROTOCOL. February 19, 1904.
Signed by Ecuador's Minister of Foreign Relations
Dr. Valverde, and Minister Plenipotentiary (of Peru)
Mariano H. Cornejo. Both parties informed the King
of Spain that they wanted him to proceed with the arbi-
tration which had been suspended (See GARCIA-HE-
RRERA TREATY), and to appoint a commission to study
the material bearing upon the boundary issue. The
king accepted the role of arbitrator and sent Ramón
Menéndez Pidal as his special commissioner to South
America.

VANGUARDIA SOCIALISTA REVOLUCIONARIA ECUATORI-
ANA (VSRE). A militant splinter group which developed out of the Socialist Party in 1930. The Vanguard was led by General Luis Larrea Alba, who was
put up as their presidential candidate in the 1936
election. Larrea Alba's presidential aspirations failed
and the Vanguard disintegrated soon thereafter.

VARGAS, JOSE MARIA. Born, November 9, 1902, Chorde-
leg, cantón Gualaceo, Azuay. Historian of Ecuadorean

art and folklore, especially of the colonial period. Member of the Dominican Order.

VARGAS TORRES, LUIS. Born, Esmeraldas. Died, March 20, 1887, Cuenca. Led some of Eloy Alfaro's forces against the Veintimilla dictatorship in 1882. Later participated in uprising against Veintimilla's successor, José María Plácido Caamaño. He was captured and executed March 20, 1887 at Cuenca. In 1897 his remains were transported by the Alfaro regime to a hero's burial in Guayaquil.

VASQUEZ, JUAN BAUTISTA. Born, Cuenca. Died, May 24, 1899. Education: J. D., University of Azuay. Politician, lawyer. Participated in constitutional convention of 1852 and 1878.

VASQUEZ DE VELASCO, PEDRO. Born, Palencia, 1603. Died, Chuquisaca, 1670. Public official. District attorney of Guatemala, 1637; criminal lawyer of same; district attorney of Lima, 1647; president of the Audiencia of Quito, 1655-61; president of the Audiencia of Charcas, 1661-70. He advocated the abolition of the mita, a reform not effected until after independence.

VASQUEZ OCHOA, HONORATO. Born, May 28, 1855, Cuenca. Died, January 26, 1932, Cuenca. Statesman, diplomat. One of the most prolific writers of Ecuador whose bibliography comprises 297 different titles. One of his most important works is entitled Memoria histórica-jurídica sobre límites, 1892. As a statesman, he was Ecuador's envoy to Spain in 1870 representing his country's interests over the border question with Peru.

VEINTIMILLA, IGNACIO DE. Born, July 31, 1828, Quito. Died, July 19, 1908, Quito. Education: Colegio Militar, Quito. Soldier, politician. Minister of War, 1865-67; inspector of the Army, 1866; brigadier general, 1867; commanding general of Guayaquil. Presidency: (1) non-elected, age 48, 1876, overthrew President Antonio Borrero; (2) elected (Constituent Convention), age 50, 1878, one term, proclaimed dictatorship; (3) non-elected, age 54, 1882, overthrown in 1883.

VEINTIMILLA, JOSE DE. Born, 1823, Quito. Died, March

19, 1869, Guayaquil. Soldier. Father of Doña Marietta de Veintimilla de LaPierre. He left his university
studies to enter military school, rose to the rank of
brigadier general under Urbina, and died in battle during the civil disturbances of 1869.

VEINTIMILLA DE GALINDO, DOLORES. Born, Quito, 1829.
Died, May, 1857. Poet and early defender of the
rights of women. Opponent of capital punishment.
She became so exasperated with the evils of the society in which she found herself that she took her own
life, burning all but a few of her rather extensive
poetic compositions beforehand.

VEINTIMILLA DE LAPIERRE, MARIETTA DE. Born,
September 8, 1858. Died, March 11, 1907, Quito.
Feminist. Writer for many newspapers and magazines
in her own country and especially abroad, she was
an active participant in politics. Daughter of General
José de Veintimilla, and niece of General Ignacio de
Veintimilla, she assumed command of the military
forces in Quito in her uncle's absence, thereby earn-
ing the nickname, "La Generalita." After a valiant
effort to prevent loss of the garrison and the city to
the opponents of her uncle, often under full exposure
to hostile fire, she was finally arrested on January 11,
1883, and remained in jail until September 2, when
she was finally released and allowed to leave the country after the fall of the Veintimilla dictatorship. Her
Páginas del Ecuador, a book of memoirs, was published in Lima in 1890, and caused lively controversy.
Her husband, Antonio LaPierre, died soon after their
marriage, when she was under 20 years of age.

VELA HERVAS, JUAN BENIGNO. Born, 1843, Ambato.
Died, February 24, 1920, Ambato. Jurisconsult,
writer, parliamentarian. Co-author of the 1906 Constitution, governor of Tungurahua Province.

VELASCO IBARRA, JOSE MARIA. Born, March 19, 1893,
Quito. Education: J.D., University of Quito. Lawyer, university professor, politician. Deputy from
Pichincha Province, 1932; president of the Chamber
of Deputies, 1933. Presidency: (1) elected (popular),
age 41, 1934, one term, resigned in 1935; (2) non-
elected, age 51, 1944, ushered in by revolution;
(3) elected (Constituent Convention), age 52, 1944,

one term, proclaimed dictatorship; (4) non-elected
(assumed dictatorial power), age 53, 1946, overthrown
in 1947; (5) elected (popular), age 59, 1952, one term,
which ended constitutionally in 1956; (6) elected (popular) age 67, 1960, one term, overthrown in 1961;
(7) elected (popular) age 75, 1968, one term, (assumed
dictatorial power in 1970); overthrown by the military,
February 15, 1972. At present living in exile in
Buenos Aires.

VELASCO Y PEREZ PETROCHE, JUAN MANUEL DE, S. J.
Born, January 6, 1727, Riobamba. Died, June 29,
1792, in exile, Faenza, Italy. Entered the Society of
Jesus, July 23, 1746. Studied at the Jesuit College
of Quito. Historian. La historia moderna del Reino
de Quito.

VELEZ, JOSE MIGUEL. Born, July, 1829, Cuenca. Died,
December 1, 1892, Cuenca. Sculptor of considerable
fame. Winner of a number of awards for his busts of
prominent Ecuadoreans of his time.

VENEGAS CAÑAVERAS, PEDRO. Died, 1586. Public official. Acting president of the Audiencia of Quito, 1581-
87. He occupied the presidency in the interim between
the death of Don Juan Martínez de Landecho, who died
in Panamá in 1581 on the way to take over the office,
until the arrival of Don Manuel Barros de San Millán,
August 2, 1587.

VERA, PEDRO JORGE. Born, June 16, 1914, Guayaquil.
Journalist, novelist. He was minister of Education,
1944; co-founder of the magazine, La Calle, and founder
of the political magazines, Mañana and Ecuador 70.
Author: Los animales puros (novel), 1946; La guamo-
teña (novel), 1946; Luto eterno y otros relatos, 1953.

VILLACIS, ANIBAL. Born, 1927, Ambato. Studied in
Paris and Spain. Contemporary painter.

VILLAGOMEZ, JOSE A. Born, 189?, Guayaquil. Physician, publicist, and poet. A member of the Modernist movement. Literary critic and writer in numerous newspapers and journals, he was a founder of El
Telégrafo Literario, an important mouthpiece for his
own ideas and those of several others. He is a

physician also distinguished for his efforts in popular
health education.

VILLAGOMEZ, JUAN AURELIO. Born, June 24, 1865,
Quito. Died, September 26, 1917, Quito. Education:
J. D., Central University of Quito, 1890. Lawyer,
professor, writer, politician. Professor of law,
Central University of Quito and University of Guayaquil, 1893; Dean of Law School, Central University,
various occasions; Senator from Pichincha Province,
1915. Author: Curso elemental del derecho romano,
monografía general de la Universidad Central de Quito.
One of the most honored law professors of the Central
University of Quito.

VILLAGOMEZ DE FUROIANI, ROSARIO. Born, May 29,
1897, Quito. Educated, National School of Fine Arts,
Quito. Sculptress. Her portrait busts and public
monuments are widely distributed and equally acclaimed.

VILLALENGUA Y MAFIL, JUAN JOSE DE. Public official,
lawyer. Criminal prosecutor for Lima; President of
the Audiencia of Quito, 1784-90.

VILLAMIL, JOSE DE. Born, June 10, 1788, New Orleans,
Louisiana. Died, May 12, 1866, Guayaquil. Resident
of Louisiana when Napoleon sold the area to the
United States, he eventually joined the independence
movement in Ecuador. He fought in various cam-
paigns against Spanish domination. After 1830 he
was chief advocate of Ecuadorean occupation of the
Galápagos and became first governor of the islands.
Minister to the United States in 1852.

VILLARROEL, GASPAR DE. Born, in 1587, Riobamba.
Died, October 12, 1665, Chuquisaca, Peru. Education: University of San Agustín, Lima. Clergyman,
author, orator. Professor of theology, bishop of
Santiago, Chile, 1640; archbishop of Arequipa, Peru,
1651; archbishop of Charcas, 1655. He was the
author of an important study on Mexican and Peruvian
Indian customs. Notable as a criollo who achieved
high authority.

VILLAVICENCIO, ANTONIO DE (Conde del Real Agrado).
Born, January, 1775, Quito. Died, June 6, 1816,
Bogotá (firing squad). Involved in the independence
struggle.

VILLAVICENCIO, MANUEL. Born, in 1822, Quito. Died
  in 1871, Chile. Education: M. D., University of
  Santo Tomás, 1850. Governor of the Amazon region
  under President Urbina. Author of Geografía de la
  República del Ecuador, 1858, which is probably the
  first geographical work on the nation.

VIRINGO. In wide use with the meaning "naked" or almost
  without clothing.

VISTAZO. Monthly magazine published in Guayaquil with
  a circulation of 10, 000. It was first issued on July
  4, 1957 and has an independent editorial policy. Its
  director is Xavier Alvarado Roca.

VIVERO Y TOLEDO, LUIS FERNANDO. Born, June 5,
  1790, Pujulí. Died, October 1, 1842, Guayaquil.
  Education: doctor of theology, University of Santo
  Tomás, Quito, 1814. Writer and jurist, statesman.
  Guayaquil independence leader. Representative of
  Guayas Province in greater Colombia legislature,
  1822; associate of Olmedo (q. v.) in Guayaquil.

VOLADOR. Type of rocket much used in popular celebra-
  tions in Ecuador. The usual Spanish vocable for
  these is cohete.

VSRE see VANGUARDIA SOCIALISTA ...

- W -

W. The letter "w" does not occur in Spanish, but is used
  in some systems of transliteration of the Quechua and
  other indigenous languages, instead of the Spanish "hu"
  or "gu. " In the case of a word spelled with "w, "
  therefore, if it is included in this compilation it will
  be under "hu"; example, "wasipungo" equals "huasipungo, " etc.

WHYMPER, EDWARD. Born, April 27, 1840, London.
  Died, December 6, 1911, Chamonix. British traveler
  who was in Ecuador in 1879 and wrote Travel Amongst
  the Great Andes of the Equator, 1891. Although his
  major preoccupation was vulcanography he also wrote
  a noteworthy chapter on Ecuadorean archeology, establishing himself as a precursor in his field. He and

two Italian companions, Juan Antonio and Luis Carrel, first ascended the volcano Chimborazo in January of 1880.

WIENER, CHARLES. Born, August 25, 1851, in Austro-Hungary, of Jewish parents. Died, early December, 1913, Rio de Janeiro. Traveler, anthropologist, diplomat. As a child he went to Paris, where he was educated, and eventually naturalized as a French citizen, also becoming a Roman Catholic. Professor at the Sorbonne, 1872. Leader of an expedition to Peru, Ecuador, and Brazil, 1875-77. Vice-consul for France, Guayaquil, October 1877, and later in various diplomatic posts in Chile, Mexico and Paraguay, attaining the rank of minister plenipotentiary. The expedition of 1875-77 included a voyage from Guayaquil via Quito to Archidona, the Coca, Napo, and Marañón rivers, thence down the Amazon to Pará, Brazil, via Manaus. Wiener wrote a controversial journal of the entire expedition titled, in French, Perou et Bolivie, Récit de voyage suivi d'éstudes archéologiques et de notes sur les langues des populations indiennes (Paris, Hachette, 1880). The portion on the Ecuadorean trips has been translated and printed in Spanish. See the Bibliography under Wiener, Charles.

WOLF, TEODORO. Born, 1841. Died in 1924, Germany. German geologist and geographer who came to Ecuador in 1870 as a member of a group of scientists who were to teach in the Politechnic Institute. He remained there until 1892. His most important contribution was a book entitled Geografia y geologia del Ecuador, 1892, which remains a classic to this date.

WRIGHT, TOMAS CARLOS. Born, January 26, 1800, Queensborough House, Drogheda, Ireland. Died, December 10, 1868, Guayaquil. Military man who attained the rank of general of division in the Ecuadorean Army. As a cadet in the Royal Navy he fought in the War of 1812 against the United States. After the war he joined "Campbell's Rifles," a troop of volunteers recruited in London to fight with Bolívar for the independence of the Viceroyalty of New Granada. Wright was with Sucre when he went to Ecuador following the uprising of October 9, 1820, at Guayaquil. He participated in the campaign which began with the

insurgent victory at Chone, August 19, 1821, and ended
with the defeat of the Spanish under Aymerich at
Pichincha, May 24, 1822.   Later Wright served in the
navy of Gran Colombia, and upon the separation of
Ecuador from Gran Colombia, he settled in Guayaquil
where he served in various non-military posts, including that of governor-general of Guayas.

- X -

XIMENA, RAFAEL. Born in 1789, Guayaquil. Died,
    April 11, 1830, Lima.   Member of 1820 provisional
    council in Ecuador, Colonel in the insurgent army,
    he favored complete independence from the Colombian
    Union when the Spaniards had been defeated, and left
    Ecuador for Peru when his ideas were rejected.   He
    held important government positions there.

- Y -

YAGUACHI.   1) A major tributary of the Guayas river which
    is formed by the union of the Chimbo and Chanchán.
    2) Town on the river of the same name where the in-
    surgents under General Mires were victorious, August
    19, 1821.

YANACONA.   An Indian who worked or lived as a servant
    of the Spaniards or creoles.

YANAPERO.   An Indian whose wage or compensation consists
    of the price which he pays the owner for grazing and
    sheltering his animals on a hacienda.   The practice is
    outlawed in recent agrarian reform legislation.

YAPA.   Equivalent in Ecuador of the Mexican pilón, which in
    this sense means any extra quantity or special small
    gift given by a seller when payment is received on a
    bill or when he and a buyer make a deal.   This is a
    customary way of doing business.

YCAZA, ROSA BORJA DE. Born, July 30, 1889, Guayaquil.
    Writer and educator, feminist.   Director, Center of
    Literary Studies, University of Guayaquil.   Writer for
    the feminist cause.   Founder of the review, Nuevos

Horizontes, Guayaquil. Honored in Venezuela and
Uruguay as well in Ecuador for her efforts as an
educator.

YEROVI, JOSE MARIA DE JESUS, O. F. M. Born, Quito,
April 12, 1819. Died, Quito, June 20, 1867. Doctor
of theology, University of Santo Tomás, Quito. Clergyman, member of the Franciscan order. He was elected fourth archbishop of Quito in 1867, but died soon
thereafter.

YEROVI INDABURO, CLEMENTE. Born, August, 1904,
Barcelona, Spain. Education: Colegio San Gabriel,
Quito, some university training. Economist, banker.
President of the Chamber of Agriculture, Guayaquil;
director of the Central Bank of Ecuador; senator;
Ecuadorean ambassador to the European Common
Market, and many other positions of developmental
and civic character. Presidency: non-elected, age
62, 1966. He was appointed by Ecuador's political
party leaders after the abdication of the governing
military junta.

YUMBO   The Yumbo descended from the Panzaleo tribe
and lived on the western slope of the Andes next to
the Cayapa Indians during the Spanish conquest. The
term Yumbo applies today to most lowland Indians, and
has no ethnic value. Yumbo is presently applied to
the Quechua-speaking Indians of the Oriente. They
number about 40, 000 and live primarily in the larger
settlements, such as Napo, Tena, Puyo, Archidona and
Baeza.

- Z -

ZABALA BAQUERIZO, JORGE. Born, March 13, 1922,
Guayaquil. Education: J. D. , University of Guayaquil,
1946. Professor of philosophy, psychology and logic
at the Aguirre Abad High School in Guayaquil, 1947;
professor of law, University of Guayaquil, 1959; substitute deputy from Guayas Province, 1958; vice-president of the republic, 1968. Member of the Radical
Liberal Party; supported the left-wing Parra-Carrión
ticket in the 1960 presidential election.

ZALDUMBIDE, GONZALO. Born in 1884, Quito. Died,

1881. Gentleman farmer, man of letters, public official, diplomat, poet. Deputy in the National Congress, 1864-1868. Minister of Public Instruction, ambassador to Colombia, candidate for the presidency. Zaldumbide participated in the best period of Romanticism. His extensive poetic works have not been collected, since they were published in magazines and newspapers of his time. He translated Byron and other poets.

ZAMORA. Capital of the province of Zamora-Chinchipe. Population (1968 est.), less than 10,000.

ZAMORA-CHINCHIPE. Southernmost Ecuadorean province in the Oriente region. Prior to November 10, 1953, Zamora-Chinchipe formed one province with Morona-Santiago. Total area of the two provinces is 18,358 square miles. Separate figures are unavailable. Population (1968 est.), 15,900.

ZANGURIMA, GASPAR. Born, Cuenca, August 16, 1787. Died, Cuenca, 1823. Artist and artisan, equally famous for his religious art and the making of guitars and violins. He was nicknamed "Lluqui" for his left handedness. His two sons, Cayetano and José María, were brought up to collaborate in his work. He was supporter of the independence movement and once the province of Azuay was freed, the governor, Tomás de Heres, ordained the establishment of a school of fine arts with Zangurima as director, but before it could get under way Zangurima died.

ZARUMA. Town in the Province of El Oro, head of the canton of the same name. An excellent grade of quality coffee takes its name from Zaruma.

ZARUMILLA-CHACRAS, BATTLE OF. July 25, 1941. Highlighted an undeclared but real war between Ecuador and Peru begun in 1941. In the battle, the Peruvian Colonel Manuel Odría decisively defeated the Ecuadorean forces. This led to the signing of the Protocol of Rio de Janeiro (q.v.) on January 29, 1942.

ZELAYA Y VERGARA, JUAN ANTONIO DE. Public official. President of the Audiencia of Quito, September, 1766 to July 7, 1767.

ZURRON.   Leather sack in which cocoa beans were exported.

Appendix 1

KINGDOM OF THE SCYRIS AT QUITO, 980-1300

Scyris de Carán: 11 of them reigned 320 years, from 980 to 1300.

Name	Reign	(Years)
Toa and Duchicela (Scyri 12th)	1300 to 1370	70 years
Autachi Duchicela (Scyri 13th)	1370 to 1430	60 years
Hualcopo Duchicela (Scyri 14th)	1430 to 1463	33 years
Cacha Duchicela (Scyri 15th)	1463 to 1487	24 years
Paccha and Huayna Cápac (16th)	1487 to 1525	38 years
Atahualpa (17th)	1525 to 1533	8 years
Hualpa Cápac (18th)	1533	2 months
Rumiñahui	1533 to 1534	1 year, 5 months

Appendix 2

CHRONOLOGY OF THE INCAS, 1021-1571

Name	Reign		(Years)
MANCOCAPAC I	1021 to 1062	(died)	40 years
SINCHI ROCA	1062 to 1091	(died)	30 years
LLOQUE YUPANQUI	1091 to 1126	(died)	35 years
MAITA CAPAC	1126 to 1156	(died)	30 years
CAPAC YUPANQUI	1156 to 1197	(died)	41 years
INCA ROCA	1197 to 1249	(died)	51 years
YAGUAR GUACAC	1249 to 1289		40 years[a]
VIRACOCHA	1289 to 1340	(died)	51 years
INCA URCO	1340 to 1340	(died)[b]	
PACHACUTEC	1340 to 1400	(died)	60 years
YUPANQUI	1400 to 1439	(died)	39 years
TUPAC YUPANQUI	1439 to 1475	(died)	36 years
HUAYNA CAPAC	1475 to 1525	(died)	50 years
HUASCAR	1526 to 1532	(died)	7 years
ATAHUALPA	1532 to 1533	(died)	14 months
MANCO CAPAC	1535 to 1553		20 years[c]
SAYRI TUPAC	1553 to 1559		7 years[d]
CUSITITO YUPANQUI	1563 to 1569	(died)	6 years
TUPAC AMARU	1569 to 1571	(died)	3 years[e]

---

a. Died in 1296. Renounced the crown and ceded it to her
   son, Viracocha.
b. Reigned 11 days.
c. Crowned by Francisco Pizarro.
d. Abdicated in 1559.
e. Reigned a scant 3 years.

Appendix 3

BISHOPS OF THE CITY OF QUITO, 1545-1849

Creation of the Diocese: 8 January 1545

Dr. Garci Díaz Arias	8 January	1550--1562
Fray Pedro de la Peña, O. P.	27 April	1566--1582
Fray Antonio de San Miguel and Solier, O. F. M.	10 October	1587--1590a
Fray Luis López de Solís, O. S. A.	25 June	1594--1606
Dr. Andrés Pérez		1606b
Fray Salvador de Ribera, O. P.	14 March	1607--1612
Dr. Fernando Arias de Ugarte	6 January	1614--1615
Fray Alfonso de Santillana, O. P.	June	1617--1622
Fray Francisco de Sotomayor, O. F. M.	30 January	1625--1629
Fray Pedro de Oviedo, Cits.	17 January	1630c--1646
Dr. Agustín de Ugarte y Saravia	9 November	1647--1650
Dr. Alfonso de la Peña	December	1653--1687
Dr. Sancho de Andrade y Figueroa	1 April	1688--1702
Dr. Diego Ladrón de Guevara	31 October	1702--1710
Dr. Luis Francisco de Romero		1718--1726
Dr. Juan Gómez de Nava y Frías	October	1726--1729
Dr. Juan de Escandón		1731d
Dr. Andrés de Paredes Polanco y Armendáriz		1734--1745
Dr. Juan Nieto Polo del Aguila		1748--1759
Dr. Pedro Ponce y Carrasco	1 September	1764--1775

Dr. Blas Sobrino y Minayo	18 September	1776--1789
Dr. José Pérez Calama	26 February	1791--1792
Fray José Díaz de la Madrid, O. F. M.	July	1793--1794
Dr. Miguel Alvaro Cortés	2 July	1796--1799
Dr. José Cuero y Caicedo		1800--1815
Fray Miguel Fernández, O. F. M.		1816[e]
Dr. Leonardo Santander y Villavicencio		1817--1822[f]
Dr. Manuel de Los Santos Escobar		1827--1828
Dr. Rafael Lasso de la Vega		1828--1833
Dr. Nicolás Joaquín de Arteta y Calisto		1833--1849

a. Died in Riobamba, December 7, 1590, when on his way to Quito to take charge of his office. He did not occupy it.
b. Did not take possession
c. Late in 1646
d. Was designated archbishop of Lima, thus personally never taking office.
e. Did not take possession.
f. Retired right after the victory of Pichincha.

Appendix 4

ARCHBISHOPS OF THE CITY OF QUITO, 1849-(1973)

Creation of the Diocese: 13 January 1849

Dr. Nicolás Joaquín de Arteta y Celiato	1849--1851
Dr. Francisco Javier de Garaycoa	1851--1861
Dr. José María Riofrio	1861--1867
Fray José M. Yerovi, O. F. M.	1867--1868
Dr. José Ignacio Checa y Barba	1868--1882a
Dr. José Ignacio Ordóñez	1882--1893
Dr. Pedro Rafael González y Calisto	1893--1906
Dr. Federico González Suárez	1906--1917
Dr. Manuel María Pólit Laso	1919--1933
Cardenal Carlos María de la Torre	1933--1967
Dr. Pablo Muñoz Vega, S. J.	1967--

---

a. Died poisoned.

PRESIDENTS OF THE REAL AUDIENCIA, 1564-1822

Hernando de Santillán	18 September	1564--1568
Lope Aux Díez de Armendáriz	19 July	1571--1574
N. García de Valverde	11 August	1575--1578
Diego de Narváez	2 June	1578--1581
Pedro Venegas Cañaveras		1581--1587[a]
Manuel Barros de San Millán	2 August	1587--1593
Miguel de Ibarra	5 February	1600--1608
Juan Fernández de Recalde		1609--1612
Antonio de Morga	21 August	1615--1636
Alonso Pérez de Salazar		1637--1642
Juan de Lizárazu		1642--1645
Martín de Arriola		1647--1652
Pedro Vásquez de Velasco		1655--1661
Juan Antonio Fernández de Heredia		1661[b]
Diego del Corro Carrascal		1670--1673
Alonso de la Peña Montenegro		1674--1678
Lope Antonio de Munive y Aspee		1678--1689
Mateo de la Mata Ponce de León	20 January	1691--1701
Francisco López Dicastillo	28 August	1703--1705[c]
Juan de Sosaya	May	1707--1714
Santiago de Larraín	28 July	1715--1718
Santiago de Larraín		1722--1728
Dionisio de Alcedo y Herrera	20 September	1728--1736
José de Araujo y Río	28 December	1736--1743
Francisco Miguel de Goyeneche		1741[d]
Fernando Félix Sánchez de Orellana	12 March	1745--1753
Juan Pío de Montúfar	22 September	1753--1761[e]
Juan Antonio de Zelaya y Vergara	September	1766--1767[f]
José Diguja	17 July	1767--1778
José García de León y Pizarro	23 November	1778--1784
Juan José de Villalengua y Marfil		1784--1790

Juan Antonio Mon y Velarde	29 April	1790--1791
Luis Antonio Muñoz de Guamán		1791--1798
Luis Francisco Héctor, Barón de Carondelet	2 February	1798--1806
Manuel Urriez, Conde de Ruíz de Castilla	1 August	1808--1811
Juan Pío Montúfar		1809
Toribio Montes	7 November	1812--1817
Juan Ramírez de Orozco	26 July	1817-1819
Juan de la Cruz Murgeón	24 December	1821--1822
Melchor Aymerich	April	1822--1822g

---

a. Followed from 1581 to 1587, the Oidor Pedro Venegas Cañaveras.
b. He died before taking possession.
c. At the end of the year 1705.
d. He resigned the charge in favor of Fernando Félix Sánchez de Orellana. He did not take possession.
e. Died.
f. Interim. Was governor of the District of Guayaquil.
g. Until May 24, 1822.

Appendix 6

CONSTITUTIONS OF ECUADOR: 1830-(1973)

No.	(Promulgation Date)	City in Which Promulgated	Time in Effect (yr) (mth) (dy)		
1	(September 23, 1830)	Riobamba	4	10	20
2	(August 13, 1835)	Ambato	7	7	17
3	(April 1, 1843)	Quito	2	8	3
4	(December 3, 1845)	Cuenca	5	2	22
5	(February 25, 1851)	Quito	1	6	11
6	(September 6, 1852)	Guayaquil	8	3	4
7	(March 10, 1861)	Quito	8	2	29
8	(June 9, 1869)	Quito	8	9	27
9	(April 9, 1878)	Ambato	5	9	28
10	(February 4, 1884)	Quito	12	11	10
11	(January 14, 1896)	Quito	10	11	9
12	(December 23, 1906)	Quito	22	3	3
13	(March 26, 1929)	Quito	14	11	9
14	(March 5, 1945)	Quito	--	9	25
15	(December 31, 1946)	Quito	20	4	25
16	(May 25, 1967)	Quito	presently in effect		

Appendix 7

ECUADOREAN CHIEF EXECUTIVES, 1830-(1973)

Chief Executive (Method of Election)	From		To	
Juan José Flores (1b)	May 13,	1830--Jan.	18,	1835
Vicente Rocafuerte (3)	Jan. 18,	1835--Aug.	1,	1835
Vicente Rocafuerte (1b)	Aug. 1,	1835--Jan.	31,	1839
Juan José Flores (1b)	Jan. 31,	1839--Jan.	18,	1843
Provisional Junta (3)	Jan. 18,	1843--Mar.	31,	1843
Juan José Flores (1b)	Mar. 31,	1843--Mar.	6,	1845*
Provisional Junta (3)	Mar. 6,	1845--Dec.	8,	1845
Vicente Ramón Roca (1b)	Dec. 8,	1845--Oct.	15,	1849
Manuel de Ascásubi (3)	Oct. 15,	1849--Feb.	20,	1850
Diego Noboa (3)	Feb. 20,	1850--Feb.	25,	1851
Diego Noboa (1b)	Feb. 25,	1851--July	17,	1851*
José María Urbina (3)	July 17,	1851--Aug.	31,	1852
José María Urbina (1b)	Aug. 31,	1852--July	13,	1856
Francisco Robles (1b)	July 13,	1856--May	1,	1859*
Provisional Junta (3)	May 1,	1859--Sept.	17,	1859
Guillermo Franco (3)	Sept. 17,	1859--Sept.	24,	1860
Provisional Junta (3)	Sept. 24,	1860--April	2,	1861
Gabriel García Moreno (1b)	April 2,	1861--Sept.	5,	1865
Jerónimo Carrión (1b)	Sept. 5,	1865--Nov.	6,	1867*
P. J. de Arteta y Calisto (2)	Nov. 6,	1867--Jan.	20,	1868
Javier Espinoza (1a)	Jan. 20,	1868--Jan.	17,	1869*
Gabriel García Moreno (3)	Jan. 17,	1869--Aug.	29,	1869
Gabriel García Moreno (1b)	Aug. 29,	1869--Aug.	6,	1875*
Francisco Javier León (2)	Aug. 6,	1875--Nov.	12,	1875
Antonio Borrero (1a)	Nov. 12,	1875--Dec.	18,	1876*
Ignacio de Veintimilla (3)	Dec. 18,	1876--Mar.	31,	1878
Ignacio de Veintimilla (1b)	Mar. 31,	1878--Mar.	26,	1882*
Ignacio de Veintimilla (3)	Mar. 26,	1882--July	9,	1883
Provisional Junta (3)	July 9,	1883--Feb.	10,	1884
J. M. P. Caamaño y Cornejo (1b)	Feb. 10,	1884--July	1,	1888
Antonio Flores Jijón (1a)	July 1,	1888--Aug.	31,	1892

Luis Cordero (1a)	Sept. 1,	1892--Apr.	16, 1895*
Vicente Lucio Salazar (2)	Apr. 16,	1895--June	18, 1895
Eloy Alfaro (3)	June 18,	1895--Jan.	12, 1897
Eloy Alfaro (1b)	Jan. 13,	1897--Aug.	31, 1901
Leónidas Plaza Gutiérrez (1a)	Sept. 1,	1901--Aug.	31, 1905
Lizardo García (1a)	Sept. 1,	1905--Jan.	15, 1906*
Eloy Alfaro (3)	Jan. 16,	1906--Jan.	1, 1907
Eloy Alfaro (1b)	Jan. 2,	1907--Aug.	11, 1911*
Carlos Freile Zaldumbide (2)	Aug. 11,	1911--Aug.	31, 1911
Emilio Estrada (1a)	Sept. 31,	1911--Dec.	22, 1911*
Carlos Freile Zaldumbide (2)	Dec. 22,	1911--Aug.	31, 1912
Francisco Andrade Marin (2)	Mar. 6,	1912--Aug.	31, 1912
Leónidas Plaza Gutiérrez (1a)	Sept. 1,	1912--Aug.	31, 1916
Alfredo Baquerizo Moreno (1a)	Sept. 1,	1916--Aug.	31, 1920
José Luis Tamayo (1a)	Sept. 1,	1920--Aug.	31, 1924
Gonzalo S. Córdova (1a)	Sept. 1,	1924--July	9, 1925*
Provisional Junta (3)	July 9,	1925--April	1, 1926
Isidro Ayora (3)	April 1,	1926--Mar.	25, 1929
Isidro Ayora (1b)	Mar. 26,	1929--Aug.	24, 1931*
Luis Larrea Alba (2)	Aug. 24,	1931--Oct.	15, 1931
Alfredo Baquerizo Moreno (2)	Oct. 15,	1931--Aug.	27, 1932
Carlos Freile Larrea (2)	Aug. 27,	1932--Sept.	2, 1932
Alberto Guerrero Martínez (2)	Sept. 2,	1932--Dec.	4, 1932
J. de Dios Martínez Mera (1a)	Dec. 5,	1932--Oct.	20, 1933*
Abelardo Montalvo (2)	Oct. 20,	1933--Aug.	31, 1934
José María Velasco Ibarra (1a)	Sept. 1,	1934--Aug.	20, 1935*
Antonio Pons (2)	Aug. 21,	1935--Sept.	26, 1935
Federico Páez (3)	Sept. 26,	1935--Oct.	22, 1937
Alberto Enríquez Gallo (3)	Oct. 23,	1937--Aug.	10, 1938
Manuel María Borrero (2)	Aug. 10,	1938--Dec.	2, 1938
Aurelio Mosquera Narváez (1a)	Dec. 2,	1938--Nov.	17, 1939*
Carlos A. Arroyo del Río (2)	Nov. 17,	1939--Dec.	10, 1939
Andrés Córdova Nieto (2)	Dec. 11,	1939--Aug.	31, 1940
Julio E. Moreno (2)	Aug. 10,	1940--Aug.	31, 1940
Carlos A. Arroyo del Río (1a)	Sept. 1,	1940--May	28, 1944*

Provisional Junta (3)	May 28, 1944--May	31, 1944
José María Velasco Ibarra (3)	June 1, 1944--Aug.	10, 1944
José María Velasco Ibarra (1b)	Aug. 10, 1944--Mar.	30, 1946*
José María Velasco Ibarra (3)	Mar. 30, 1946--Aug.	23, 1947
Carlos Mancheno Cajas (3)	Aug. 23, 1947--Sept.	2, 1947
Mariano Suárez Veintimilla (2)	Sept. 2, 1947--Sept.	17, 1947
C. Julio Arosemena Tola (1b)	Sept. 17, 1947--Aug.	31, 1948
Galo Plaza Lasso (1a)	Sept. 1, 1948--Aug.	31, 1952
José María Velasco Ibarra (1a)	Sept. 1, 1952--Aug.	31, 1956
Camilo Ponce Enríquez (1a)	Sept. 1, 1956--Aug.	31, 1960
José María Velasco Ibarra (1a)	Sept. 1, 1960--Nov.	9, 1961*
C. Julio Arosemena Monroy (2)	Nov. 9, 1961--July	11, 1963
Provisional Junta (3)	July 11, 1963--Mar.	29, 1966
Clemente Yerovi Indaburo (3)	Mar. 30, 1966--Nov.	15, 1966
Otto Arosemena Gómez (1b)†	Nov. 16, 1966--Aug.	31, 1968
José María Velasco Ibarra (1a)	Sept. 1, 1968--June	22, 1970*
José María Velasco Ibarra (1b)	June 22, 1970--Feb.	15, 1972*
Guillermo Rodríguez Lara (3)	Feb. 15, 1972--	

This table does not include regional rulers nor the vice-presidents who assumed office temporarily because the incumbent was either out of the country or physically handicapped.

Method of Election: 1a. Direct, popular election
1b. Indirect election
2. Acting or interim president
3. Extra-constitutional president

*Did not complete term.
†Elected for an interim period by the Congress.

171

Appendix 8

PROVINCES AND CANTONS

In their geographical order, north to south: by regions: Sierra, Costa, and Oriente.

Provinces (and Capitals)	Cantons (and Centers of Government)
CARCHI (Tulcán)	Tulcán (same) Montúfar (San Gabriel) Espejo (El Angel)
IMBABURA (Ibarra)	Otavalo (same) Cotacachi (same) Antonio Ante (Atuntaquí)
PICHINCHA (Quito)	Quito (same) Cayambe (same) Pedro Moncayo (Tabacundo) Mejía (Machachi) Rumiñahui (Sangolquí)
COTOPAXI (Latacunga)	Latacunga (same) Salcedo (San Miguel de Salcedo) Pujilí (same) Pangua (El Corazón) Saquisilí (same)
TUNGURAHUA (Ambato)	Ambato (same) Pelileo (same) Píllaro (same) Baños (same)
CHIMBORAZO (Riobamba)	Riobamba (same) Guano (same) Colta (Cajabamba) Alausí (same) Guamote (same) Chunchi (same)

Provinces (and Capitals)	Cantons (and Centers of Government)
BOLIVAR (Guaranda)	Guaranda (same) Chimbo (San José de Chimbo) San Miguel (San Miguel de Bolívar)
CAÑAR (Azogues)	Azogues (same) Cañar (same) Biblián (same)
AZUAY (Cuenca)	Cuenca (same) Gualaceo (same) Paute (same) Girón (same) Sigsig (same) Santa Isabel (same)
LOJA (Loja)	Loja (same) Saraguro (same) Gonzanamá (same) Paltas (Catacocha) Celica (same) Calvas (Cariamanga) Puyango (Alamor) Macará (same)
ESMERALDAS (Esmeraldas)	Esmeraldas (same) Eloy Alfaro (Valdez) Muisne (same)
MANABI (Portoviejo)	Montecristi (same) Manta (same) Jipijapa (same) Rocafuerte (same) Santa Ana (same) Sucre (Bahía de Caráquez) Junín (same) Paján (same) Chone (same) Bolívar (Calceta) 24 de Mayo (Sucre)
LOS RIOS (Babahoyo)	Babahoyo (same) Baba (same) Vinces (same)

Provinces (and Capitals)	Cantons (and Centers of Government)
	Quevedo (same) Puebloviejo (same) Ventanas (same) Urdaneta (Catarama)
GUAYAS (Guayaquil)	Guayaquil (same) Samborondón (same) Yaguachi (Yaguachi Nuevo) Daule (same) Balzar (same) Santa Elena (same) Milagro (same) Salinas (same)
EL ORO (Machala)	Machala (same) Santa Rosa (same) Arenillas (same) Zaruma (same) Pasaje (same) Piñas (same)
NAPO-PASTAZA (Tena)	Napo (Tena) Quijos (Baeza) Sucumbíos (Sta. Rosa de Sucumbíos) Aguarico (Nuevo Rocafuerte) Pastaza (Puyo)
MORONA-SANTIAGO (Macas)	Morona (Macas) Gualaquiza (same) Santiago (Méndez) Limón-Indanza (Gral. Leónidas Plaza)
ZAMORA-CHINCHIPE (Zamora)	Zamora (same) Chinchipe (Zumba) Yacuambí (same)
GALAPAGOS (Puerto Baquerizo)	

BIBLIOGRAPHY

1. BOOKS AND MONOGRAPHS

Acosta Solís, Misael. Los recursos naturales del Ecuador
y su conservación. Mexico D. F., Instituto Panameri-
cano de Geografía e Historia, 1968, 127 pp.

Albornoz, Oswaldo. Historia de la acción clerical en el
Ecuador, desde la conquista hasta nuestros días.
Quito, Editorial Espejo, 1963, 301 pp.

Alfaro, Olmedo. El asesinato de Alfaro ante la historia y
la civilización. Guayaquil, Jouvín, 1938, VII, 288 pp.

Andrade, Manuel de Jesús. Ecuador. Próceres de la independencia. Quito, 1909, 418 pp.

_____. Páginas de sangre o los asesinatos de Quito.
El 28 de enero de 1912. Panamá, Tip. "Diario de
Panamá," 1912, 120 pp.

Andrade, Roberto. Campaña de veinte días. Quito, Tip.
Escuela de Artes y Oficios, 1908, VI, 277 pp.

_____. ¡Sangre! ¿quién la derramó? Historia de los
últimos crímenes cometidos en la nación del Ecuador.
Quito, Imp. Antigua de El Quiteño Libre, 1912, 219 pp.

Arboleda R., Gustavo. Diccionario biográfico de la República del Ecuador. Quito, Tipografía de la Escuela de
Artes y Oficios, 1910, VIII, 151 pp.

Arcos, Gualberto. Años de oprobio. Quito, Imp. Fernández,
1940, 303 pp.

Arias, Augusto. Panorama de la literatura ecuatoriana. 3a.
edición. Quito, Imp. del Ministerio de Educación,
n. d. [1956], 405 pp.

Arroyo del Río, Alberto. Bajo el imperio de odio. 2 Vols.
Bogotá, Editorial Gráfico, 1946.

Barrera I., Ricardo. Descalificación presidencial. El
Congreso de 1932. Quito, Talleres Gráficos Minerva,
1950, 314 pp.

Beals, Ralph Leon. Community in Transition: Nayón,
Ecuador. Los Angeles, University of California
Press, 1966, 233 pp.

Bell, Robert E. Archeological Investigations at the Site of
El Inga, Ecuador. Quito, Casa de la Cultura Ecuatoriana, 1965, 330 pp.

Bialek, Robert. Catholic Politics. A History Based on
Ecuador. New York, Vantage Press, 1963, 144 pp.

Blanksten, George I. Ecuador: Constitutions and Caudillos.
Berkeley, University of California Press, 1951, XII,
196 pp.

Borja, Luis Alberto. Los condorazos. Buenos Aires,
Ediciones Peuser, 1954, 203 pp.

Borja y Borja, Ramiro. Derecho constitucional ecuatoriano.
3 Vols. Madrid, Ediciones Cultura Hispánica, 1950.

Borrero, Manual María. España en Quito. Quito, Editorial
Fray Jodoco Ricke, 1969, 472 pp.

_____. Quito, luz de América. Quito, Editorial "Ru-
miñahui," 1959, XIII, 338 pp.

Bossano, Luis. Apuntes acerca del regionalismo en el
Ecuador. Quito, La Prensa Católica, 1930, 178 pp.

Brooks, Rhoda S. The Barrios of Manta. New York, New
American Library, 1965, X, 366 pp.

Bruchez, Augusto. La azucena de Quito o la beata Mariana
de Jesús Paredes y Flores. Friburgo de Brisconia,
Alemania, B. Herder, 1908, 320 pp.

Carvalho-Neto, Paulo de. Diccionario del folklore ecuatoriano. Quito, Casa de la Cultura Ecuatoriana, 1964,
489 pp.

Cevallos García, Gabriel. __Entonces fue el Ecuador.__ Cuenca, Edit. Austral, 1942, 218 pp.

_____. __Reflexiones sobre la historia del Ecuador.__ 2 Vols, Cuenca, Casa del la Cultura Ecuatoriana, 606 pp., 517 pp.

_____. __Teoría del hombre-pueblo.__ Cuenca, Publicaciones de la Municipalidad, 1944, 41 pp. See also his Visión teórica del Ecuador, Puebla, Mexico, J. M. Cajica, Jr., 1960. (In the Biblioteca ecuatoriana mínima. La colonia y la república.)

Collier, John and Aníbal Buitrón. __The Awakening Valley.__ Chicago, University of Chicago Press, 1949, VII, 199 pp.

Concha Enríquez, Pedro. __Realidad. Crítica a la política contemporánea del Ecuador.__ Quito, Imp. Fernández, 1940, 131 pp.

Cordero, Luis. __Diccionario quichua-español, español quichua.__ Quito, Casa de la Cultura Ecuatoriana, 1955, XLII, 430 pp.

_____. __Enumeración botánica, Provincias de Azuay y Cañar, República del Ecuador.__ 2a. edición, Madrid, Afrodisio Aguado S. A. 1950, XVI, 254 pp.

Cornejo, Justino. __El quichua en el castellano del Ecuador.__ Publicaciones de la Academia Ecuatoriana de la Lengua. Quito, Editorial Ecuatoriana, 1967, 118 pp.

Crespo Ordóñez, Roberto. __El descubrimiento del Amazonas y los derechos territoriales del Ecuador.__ Cuenca, Ecuador, Casa de la Cultura Ecuatoriana, 1961, 55 pp.

Crespo Toral, Jorge. __El comunismo en el Ecuador.__ Quito, Librería Cultura, 1958, 62 pp.

Cuadra, José de la. __12 siluetas.__ Quito, Editorial América, 1934.

_____. __Obras completas.__ Quito, Casa de la Cultura Ecuatoriana, 986 pp.

Destruge, Camilo. __Estudios, relaciones y episodios históricos.__ Guayaquil, Tip. "El Vigilante," 1907, 270 pp.

177

Díaz Cueva, Miguel. Bibliografía de Fray Vicente Solano. Cuenca, Casa de la Cultura Ecuatoriana, Núcleo del Azuay, 1965, 318 pp.

Elizalde, Rafael H. Intereses nacionales. Necesidad de organizar los partidos políticos en el Ecuador. Santiago, Imprenta Franco-Chilena, 1913.

Endara, Carlos H. Desde el mirador de América. La dictadura y la patria nueva. Quito, Talleres Gráficos Nacionales, 1936, 45 pp.

Enock, Charles Reginald. Ecuador. New York, Charles Scribner's Sons, 1914, 375 pp.

Erickson, Edwin E., et al. Area Handbook for Ecuador. Washington, D. C., U. S. Government Printing Office, 1966, IX, 561 pp.

Espinosa Polit, Aurelio, S. J. Santa Mariana de Jesús, hija de la Compañía de Jesús. Quito, La Prensa Católica, 1957, 410 pp.

Franklin, Albert B. Ecuador: Portrait of a People. New York, Doubleday, Doran Co., 1943, VII, 326 pp.

Friede, Kurt von. Crónicas fugaces: páginas de la história ecuatoriana entre los días de 1925 a 1930. Guayaquil, Imprenta La Reforma, 1930, 592 pp.

Garcés, Enrique. Marietta de Veintimilla. Quito, Casa de la Cultura Ecuatoriana, 1949, 198 pp.

García, Leónidas. Dos capítulos de história ecuatoriana. Quito, Casa de la Cultura Ecuatoriana, 1961, 175 pp.

García Moreno, Gabriel. Defensa de los jesuitas. Quito, 1851. Guayaquil, Imp. de "La Nación," 1884, 107 pp.

García Ortíz, Humberto. La forma nacional. Quito, Imprenta de la Universidad, 1942, 384 pp.

_____. Las rutas del futuro. Quito, Casa de la Cultura, 1956, 239 pp.

Gibson, Charles Robert. Foreign Trade in the Development of Small Nations; the Case of Ecuador. New York, Frederick A. Praeger, 1971, XXII, 327 pp.

Girón, Sergio E.   La Revolución de Mayo.   Quito, Editorial
     Atahualpa, 1945.

González Páez, Miguel Angel.   Memorias históricas.   Géne-
     sis del liberalismo, su triunfo y sus obras en el
     Ecuador.   Quito, Edit. Ecuatoriana, 1934, 638 pp.

González Suárez, Federico.   Historia eclesiástica del Ecua-
     dor desde los tiempos de la conquista hasta nuestros
     días.   Quito, Imprenta del Clero, 1881, Vol. 1,
     XXXVIII, 107 pp.

Guaderas, Francisco.   Mis épocas.   Cali, Fernández y
     Lahera, 1945, 350 pp.

Guerra Borja, Marco Tulio, and Alberto Garcés Mancero.
     Conozca a los hombres de Guayaquil.   Un homenaje
     a los valores humanos de Guayaquil.   El libro de oro
     del 72.   Guayaquil, Imprenta Chonillo, C. A., 1972,
     168 pp.

Guevara, Darío C.   Las mingas en el Ecuador.   Quito,
     Editorial Universitaria, 1957, 168 pp.

Hassaurek, Friedrich.   Four Years Among Spanish-Ameri-
     cans.   London, Sampson Low, Son, and Marston,
     1868, X, 401 pp.

Hidalgo, Daniel B.   Evolución política del Ecuador.   Estudio
     histórico, jurídico y sociológico de las constituciones
     de la República del Ecuador.   Quito, 1917, 145 pp.

Icaza, Jorge.   Huasipungo.   Lima, Juan Mejía Baca and P. L.
     Villanueva, Editores, n. d. [1959].

Institute for the Comparative Study of Political Systems.
     Ecuador Election Factbook, June 2, 1968.   Washington,
     D. C., 1968.

Jacobo, Juan (Patiño, Ramón A.).   Barbaridades sin con-
     ciencia.   Quito, Editorial Rumiñahui, 1957, 191 pp.

_____.   El gran ausente.   Quito, Editorial Rumiñahui,
     1960, 208 pp.

James, Preston E.   Latin America.   3rd. edition.   New
     York, Odyssey Press, 1959.

Jaramillo Alvarado, Pío. Del agro ecuatoriano. Quito,
Imprenta de la Universidad, 1936, 348 pp.

_____. El indio ecuatoriano. 3rd. edition. Quito,
Talleres Gráficos del Estado, 1936, CIII, 227 pp.

_____. La Asamblea Liberal y sus aspectos políticos.
Quito, 1924, XLVIII, 369 pp.

Jijón y Caamaño, Jacinto. Política conservadora. Riobamba,
La Buena Prensa del Chimborazo, 1929-1934. 2 vols.

Larrea, Carlos Manuel. El Barón de Carondelet, XXIX
presidente de la Real Audiencia de Quito. Quito,
Corporación de Estudios y Publicaciones, Editorial
Fray Jodoco Ricke, 1968? 217 pp.

_____. Notas de prehistoria e historia ecuatoriana.
Quito, Editorial "Don Bosco," 1971, 370 pp.

Linke, Lilo. Ecuador, Land of Contrasts. 3rd. edition.
London, Oxford University Press, 1960, 193 pp.

Llerena, José Alfredo. Frustración política en veintidós
años. Quito, Casa de la Cultura Ecuatoriana, 1959,
113 pp.

Loor, Wilfrido. Estudios histórico-políticos. Quito,
Editorial Ecuatoriana, 1939, 335 pp.

Luna Yepés, Jorge. Explicación del ideario de ARNE.
Quito, Gráficas Sánchez, 1950, 275 pp.

_____. Síntesis histórica y geográfica del Ecuador.
Madrid, n.p., 1951, 422 pp.

_____. Visión política del Ecuador. Madrid, Ediciones
Cultura Hispánica, 1950.

Maier, Georg. The Ecuadorian Presidential Election of
June 2, 1968: An Analysis. Washington, D.C.,
Institute for the Comparative Study of Political Systems,
1969, V, 90 pp.

Maldonado Estrada, Luis. Una etapa histórica en la vida
nacional. Quito, Editorial Rumiñahui, 1954, 271 pp.

_____. Socialismo ecuatoriano: un ensayo sobre la realidad nacional. Guayaquil, Editorial "Páginas selectas" 1935.

Marz, John D. Ecuador: Conflicting Political Culture and the Quest for Progress. Boston, Allyn and Bacon, Inc., 1972, 216 pp.

Meggers, Betty J. Ecuador. New York, Frederick A. Praeger, 1966, 220 pp.

Mena Soto, Joaquín. De la dictadura militar al quinto velasquismo. Quito, Editorial Fray Jodoco Ricke, 1968, VII, 213 pp.

Miño, Ernesto. El Ecuador frente a las revoluciones proletarias. Ambato, Imprenta del Colegio Bolívar, 1935, 167 pp.

Moncayo, Pedro. El Ecuador de 1825 a 1875, sus hombres, sus instituciones y sus leyes. Santiago, 1885, 336 pp. Second edition, corrected and augmented by Carlos E. Moncayo and Luis F. Vélez. Quito, Imprenta Nacional, 1906, XXIII, 465 pp.

Monsalve Pozo, Luis. La patria y un hombre. Cuenca, Casa de la Cultura Ecuatoriana, 1961, 141 pp.

Mora Bowen, Alfonso. El liberalismo radical y su trayectoria histórica. Quito, Imprenta Romero, 1940, 283 pp.

Moreno, Julio Enrique. El sentido histórico y la cultura. Quito, Imprenta Romero, 1940, 381 pp.

Murillo Miró, Juan. Historia del Ecuador de 1876 a 1888, precedida de un resúmen histórico de 1830 a 1875. Quito, Emp. Edit. "El Comercio," 1946, 297 pp.

Needler, Martin C. Anatomy of a Coup d'Etat; Ecuador: 1963. Washington, Institute for the Comparative Study of Political Systems, 1964, V, 54 pp.

Orellana J., Gonzálo. El Ecuador en 100 años de independencia, 1830-1930. Quito, Escuela Tipográfica Salesiana, 1930, 2 Vols., VIII, 452 pp. 348 pp.

181

_____. Resúmen histórico del Ecuador. Apuntaciones cronológicas complementarias, 1947-1957. Quito, Editorial Fray Jodoco Ricke, 1948, 1957, 3 Vols.

Ortíz, Adalberto. Juyungo. Historia de un negro, una isla y otros negros. 3a. Edición. Guayaquil, Editores Librería Cervantes, 1968, 296 pp.

Páez, Federico. Explico. Quito, 1939, 118 pp.

Pareja Diezcanseco, Alfredo. Historia del Ecuador. 2 Vols. Quito, Casa de la Cultura Ecuatoriana, 1958.

_____. La lucha por la democracia en el Ecuador. Quito, Editorial Rumiñahui, 1956, 144 pp.

Parral de Velasco Ibarra, Corina. Banda presidencial. Buenos Aires, n. p., 1963, 90 pp.

Parsons, Elsie Worthington. Peguche. Canton of Otavalo, Province of Imbabura, Ecuador. A Study of Andean Indians. Chicago, University of Chicago Press, 1945, VIII, 225 pp.

Paz Larrea Alba, Clotario E. Nuestras izquierdas. Guayaquil, Imprenta Tribuna Libre, 1938, 268 pp.

Peñaherrera de Costales, Piedad and Alfredo Costales Samaniego. Historia social del Ecuador. Quito, Talleres Gráficos Nacionales, 1964, Vol. I, IIV, 372 pp.

Peralta, José. Eloy Alfaro y sus victimarios. Buenos Aires, Editorial Olimpo, 1951, 346 pp.

Pérez, F. Análisis político, social y económico de la República del Ecuador, precedida de un resúmen geográfico e histórico. Bogotá, 1858, 125 pp.

Pérez Guerrero, Alfredo. Ecuador. Quito, Casa de la Cultura Ecuatoriana, 1948, 183 pp.

Phelan, John Leddy. The Kingdom of Quito in the 17th Century. Madison, University of Wisconsin Press, 1967, XVI, 432 pp.

Plaza Lasso, Galo. Problems of Democracy in Latin America. Chapel Hill, N. C., University of North Carolina Press, 1955, 88 pp.
182

Ponce, N. Clemente. Límites entre el Ecuador y el Perú. (Boundaries between Ecuador and Perú.) Memorandum para el Ministerio de la República de Bolivia. Por N. C/P. Enviado Extraordinario y Ministro Plenipotenciario del Ecuador. 4a. Edición. Quito, Imprenta Nacional, 1936. Bilingual edition of the Memorandum of July 30, 1910.

Ponce Enríquez, Camilo. Génesis y ocaso de un régimen. Quito, Editorial "Juventud, " 1942, 85 pp.

Prescott, William H. The Conquest of Peru. London, Richard Bentley, 1857, 3 Vols.

Proaño y Vega, Eloy. Historia de la campaña del Ecuador en defensa de sus instituciones republicanas contra la dictadura del General Ignacio de Veintimilla en 1882. Quito, Imprenta de la Heredera de Pablo S. Paredes, 1884, 316 pp.

_____. Realidades ecuatorianas. Quito, Imprenta de la Universidad Central, 1938, 365 pp.

Reyes, Oscar Efrén. Historia de la república. Esquema de ideas y hechos del Ecuador a partir de la emancipación. Quito, Imprenta Nacional, 1931, 331 pp.

_____. Los últimos siete años. Quito, Talleres Gráficos Nacionales, 1933, 201 pp.

Rivera Larrea, Jorge. Veinte y siete años de velasquismo: El hombre y su ideario. Quito, Editorial Santo Domingo, 1970, 144 pp.

Robalino Dávila, Luis. Orígenes del Ecuador de hoy. Quito, Casa de la Cultura Ecuatoriana, 1966, 5 Vols.

Rubio Orbe, Gonzalo. Nuestros indios. Quito, Imprenta de la Universidad, 1947, 240 pp.

_____. La población rural ecuatoriana. Quito, Talleres Gráficos Nacionales, 1966, 308 pp.

_____. Promociones indígenas en América. Quito, Casa de la Cultura Ecuatoriana, 1957, 404 pp.

Rumazo González, Alfonso. El Congreso de 1933. Biblioteca Ecuatoriana, No. 10. Quito, Editorial Bolívar, 1934, 213 pp.

_____ . Gobernantes del Ecuador. Quito, Editorial Bolívar, 1932, 249 pp.

Sánchez Núñez, César. Del Ecuador. Fuego y sangre. Revoluciones del 11 de agosto al 6 de marzo de 1912. Bogotá, Imprenta Eléctrica, 1913, 226 pp.

Saunders, J. V. D. The People of Ecuador: A Demographic Analysis. Gainesville, University of Florida Press, 1961, 62 pp.

Silva, Dr. Rafael Euclides. Derecho territorial ecuatoriano. Guayaquil, Universidad de Guayaquil, Departamento de Publicaciones, 1962, 527 pp. and many maps.

Tamayo Mancheno, Gustavo (edit.). El velasquismo. Una interpretación poética y un violento período de lucha. Guayaquil, Editorial Royal Print, 1960, 288 pp.

Tarquino León, José. Artistas y artesanos del Azuay. Cuenca, Casa de la Cultura Ecuatoriana, Núcleo del Azuay, 1969, 142 pp.

Tobar Donoso, Julio. Monografías históricas. Quito, Editorial Ecuatoriana, 1937, 539 pp.

_____ and Alfredo Luna Tobar. Derecho territorial ecuatoriano. Quito, Editorial "La Unión Católica," 1961, 288 pp. and maps.

Torre, Carlos María de la. Catolicismo y ecuatorianidad. Quito, La Prensa Católica, 1953.

Torre Reyes, Carlos de la. La Revolución de Quito del 10 de Agosto de 1809. Quito, Ministeria de Educación, 1961.

Toscano Mateus, Humberto. El español en el Ecuador. Revista de Filología Española, Anejo LXI. Madrid, Consejo Superior de Investigaciones Científicas, 1953, 480 pp.

Troncoso, Julio C. Odio y sangre. La descalificación del Sr. Neptalí Bonifaz y la batalla de los cuatro días en Quito. Hombres y hechos de la época. Esbozo histórico-biográfico de los presidentes del Ecuador de 1830 a 1958. Quito, Editorial Fray Jodoco Ricke, 1958, 238 pp.

184

U. S. Government. Handbook of South American Indians. Vol. II. Washington, D. C., U. S. Government Printing Office, 1946.

Vaquero Dávila, Jesús. Génesis de la nacionalidad ecuatoriana. Quito, Imprenta de la Universidad, 1941, VIII, 417 pp.

Vargas, José María, O. P. Historia de la cultura ecuatoriana. Quito, Casa de la Cultura Ecuatoriana, 1965, 585 pp.

Vargas Torres, Luis. Documentos importantes para la Historia. Guayaquil, 1885.

Vargas Ugarte, Rubén, S. J. Historia del Perú. Virreinato. Vol. I, Lima, Librería e Imprenta Gil, 1949; Vol. II, Buenos Aires, Librería Stúdium, 1954; Vol. III, Lima, Librería e Imprenta Gil, 1956; Vol. IV, Buenos Aires, Librería Stúdium, 1957.

Vargas Vila, J. M. La muerte del cóndor. Buenos Aires, 1914, XI, 261 pp.

Veintimilla, Marietta de. Páginas del Ecuador. Lima, 1890.

Velasco Ibarra, José María. Caós político en el mundo contemporáneo. Buenos Aires, Américalee, 1963, 200 pp.

_____. Conciencia o barbarie. Medellín, Editorial Atlantida, 1936, 280 pp.

Vera, Alfredo. Anhelo y pasión de la democracia ecuatoriana. Guayaquil, Casa de la Cultura Ecuatoriana, 1948, 354 pp.

Villavicencio, Manuel. Geografía de la República del Ecuador. New York, Imprenta de Roberto Craighead, 1858, 505 pp.

Watkins, Ralph James. Expanding Ecuador's Exports. New York, Frederick A. Praeger, 1967, XII, 430 pp.

Whitten, Norman E. Jr. Class, Kinship, and Power in an Ecuadorean Town. The Negroes of San Lorenzo.

Stanford, California, Stanford University Press, 1965, VIII, 238 p.

Wiener, Charles. Viaje al río de las Amazonas y las cordilleras from his Perou et Bolivie, Paris, Hachette, 1880, translated and published in Viajes por América del Sur, Biblioteca Indiana, Vol. III, Madrid, Aguilar, 1958.

Wilgus, A. Curtis (ed.). Eloy Alfaro, Citizen of the Americas. Panama, Eloy Alfaro International Foundation, 1950, 68 pp.

Wolf, Teodoro. Geografía y geología del Ecuador. Leipzig, F. A. Brockhaus, 1892, XII, 671 pp.

Yépez, Manuel A. Capítulos-apuntes varios: 1830-1942. Quito, Talleres Gráficos Nacionales, 1945, 441 pp.

Zúñiga, Neptalí. Fenómenos de la realidad ecuatoriana. Quito, Talleres Gráficos de Educación, 1940, 196 pp.

2. ARTICLES; CHAPTERS IN BOOKS

Aguirre, Manuel A. "Report from Ecuador," Monthly Review, XIII, February, 1962, 456-460.

Blanksten, George I. "Caudillismo in Northern South America," South Atlantic Quarterly, LI, October, 1952, 493-537.

_____. "Political Groups in Latin America," The American Political Science Review, LIII, No. 1, March, 1959.

Borja C., Rodrigo. "Panorama de la política ecuatoriana," Combate, IV, No. 19, November and December, 1961, 16-22.

Bottomley, A. "Agricultural Employment Policy in Developing Countries; the Case of Ecuador," Inter-American Economic Affairs, XIX, Spring 1962, 53-79.

_____. "Imperfect Competition in the Industrialization of Ecuador," Inter-American Economic Affairs, XIX, Summer, 1965, 83-94.

186

Cordero Palacios, Octavio. "La muerte de don Juan Seniergues." Revista del Centro de Estudios Historicos y Geográficos. Cuenca, Entregas 11-13, December 1924-April 1928, 142-184 pp. 206; 301.

_____. "Vida de Abdón Calderón." Revista del Centro de Estudios Históricos y Geográficos, Cuenca, Entrega 3a., June, 1921, 193-220.

Costales Samaniego, Alfredo. "La tierra contra el Ecuador," Panoramas, No. 5, Mexico, September and October, 1963, 93-141.

Díaz, A. "Cambios sociales de las clases dominadas del Ecuador." Revista Mexicana de Sociología, XXV, May and August, 1963, 721-736.

Feder, Ernest. "Sobre la impotencia política de los campesinos." Revista Mexicana de Sociología, XXXI, No. 2, April and June, 1969, 323-386.

Fitzgibbon, Russel H. "The Party Potpourri in Latin America." Western Political Quarterly, X, March, 1957, 3-22.

Gold, Robert L. "Ecuador in the Era of Gabriel García Moreno: An American Assessment," in Fleener, Charles J. and Harry J. Cargas (Eds.). Religious and Cultural Factors in Latin America. St. Louis: St. Louis University, Office of International Programs, 1970.

Hamerly, M. T. "Selva Alegre, President of the Quiteña Junta of 1809: Traitor or Patriot?" Hispanic American Historical Review, 48, November, 1968, 642-653.

Heiser, Charles B., Jr. "An Illustrated Lecture on Ecuador, People, Places, Plants, and Politics," in Principal Papers, delivered at the Tenth Annual Pan American Festival, April 8-11, 1963. Latin American Institute, Southern Illinois University, Carbondale, 15-19.

Jijón y Caamaño, Jacinto. "Disertación acerca del establecimiento de la Universidad de Santo Tomás y del Real Colegio de San Fernando." Boletín de la Academia Nacional de Historia, Vol. 5, Nos. 12-14, Quito, Julio-Diciembre, 1922.

Linke, Lilo. "Ecuador's Politics: President Velasco's Fourth Exit," The World Today, XVIII, No. 2, February, 1962, 57-59.

_____. "Middle Class Life on Top of the Andes (Quito)," Central America and Mexico Quarterly Review, II, September, 1954, 47-53.

_____. "The Political Scene in Ecuador: President Velasco Ibarra Takes Over," The World Today, IX, No. 3, March, 1953, 130-133.

Maier, Georg. "The Boundary Dispute Between Ecuador and Peru," The American Journal of International Law, LXIII, January, 1969, 28-46.

_____. "A Case Study of Church-State Relations: Ecuador," in Fleener, Charles J. and Harry J. Cargas (Eds.), Religious and Cultural Factors in Latin America. St. Louis, St. Louis University, Office of International Programs, 1970.

_____. "Presidential Succession in Ecuador, 1830-1970," Journal of Inter-American Studies and World Affairs, Vol. XIII, Nos. 3 & 4, July-October, 1971, 475-509.

_____. "Structure and Political Role of Ecuador's Chambers," Specialia I, Interamericana I, Southern Illinois University, Latin American Institute, Cardondale, 1969.

Morales, Salvador. "Efimérides históricas sudamericanas," Boletín de la Sociedad Ecuatoriana de Estudios Históricos Americanos, II, No. 5 to III, No. 9, Quito, 1919.

Nett, Emily M. "Functional Elites of Ecuador," Journal of Inter-American Studies and World Affairs, XIII, January, 1971, 112-120.

_____. "The Servant Class in a Developing Country: Ecuador," Journal of Inter-American Studies, VIII, July, 1966, 437-452.

Pareja Diezcanseco, Alfredo. "Democracia y demagogia en el Ecuador," Combate, San José, Costa Rica, III, No. 15, March and April, 1961, 18-27.

_____. "Teoría y práctica del conductor conducido,"
Combate, San José, Costa Rica, IV, No. 20, January
and February, 1962, 9-23.

Preston, D. E. "Negro, Mestizo, and Indian in an Andean
Environment," Geographical Journal, 131, June, 1965,
220-234.

Rolando, Carlos A. "Los presidentes del Ecuador," Boletín del Centro de Investigaciones Históricas, IV, Nos.
4-6, Guayaquil, 1936, 234-246.

Roucek, J. S. "Ecuador in Geopolitics," Contemporary Review, 205, Fall, 1964, 74-82.

Saunders, J. V. D. "Man-Land Relations in Ecuador,"
Rural Sociology, XXVI, No. 1, March, 1961, 57-69.

Smith, Peter H. "The Image of Dictator Gabriel García
Moreno," Hispanic American Historical Review, XLV,
February, 1965, 1-24.

Times, (New York) October 10, 1911, 13 p. 5 col.,
Obituary, Archer Harman.

Times, (London) September 12, 1916, 11 p. 3 col., Obituary, Sir James Sivewright.

Wiener, Charles. "Viaje al Río de las Amazonas y las
cordilleras," from his Perou et Bolivie. Récit de
voyage suivi d'études archéologiques, et ethnographiques
et de notes sur les langues des populations indiennes.
Paris, Hachette, 1880, in Viajes por América del
Sur, Biblioteca Indiana, Madrid, Aguilar, 1958, Vol.
3.

Wright, Eduardo. "General de División Tomás Carlos
Wright," Boletín del Centro de Investigaciones Históricas, V, No. 7, Guayaquil, 1937, 412-414.

Wright, F. J. "1969 Ecuadorean Presidential Campaign,"
Inter-American Economic Affairs, XXIII, Spring 1970,
81-94.

Zuvekas, Clarence. "The Ecuadorean Economy in the 1960's,"
Business and Government Review, IX, September and
October, 1968, 11-18.

_____. "Economic Planning in Ecuador: An Evaluation, "
Inter-American Economic Affairs, XXV, No. 4, 1971,
39-69.

3.   GENERAL REFERENCE WORKS CONSULTED

Academia Nacional de Historia.   Documentos para la historia.   Vol. 1.   Quito, Imprenta de la Universidad
Central, 1922.

Arboleda R., Gustavo.   Diccionario biográfico de la República del Ecuador.   Quito, Tipografía de la Escuela
de Artes y Oficios, 1910.

Barrera, Issac J.   Próceres de la patria: lecturas biográ-
ficas.   Quito, Editorial Ecuatoriana, 1939, 180 pp.

_____.   El libro de la ciudad de San Francisco de Quito:
hasta 1950-1951.   Quito, "CEGAN," 1951.

Biblioteca Ecuatoriana Mínima.   A collection of 29 volumes,
published originally as part of the activities in connection with the Assembly of the Organization of the
American States, scheduled for 1960 at Quito, but
never held.   These volumes contain a broad selection
of materials of all sorts, literary, historical, juri-
dical, and philosophical writings from the early colonial period down to the present.   The Indices are in
the volume titled, Poesía popular, alcances, y apéndice.
Much biographical and bibliographical material not
easily found in any other one single place is included
in the collection, which however, is very uneven in
quality, each volume or section having prepared by a
different person or group of persons.   It was printed
in Mexico on the presses of J. M. Cajica, Puebla,
1960.

The Century Dictionary and Cyclopedia, Vol. IX.   Proper
Names.   New York, The Century Company, 1894-97.

Cortés, José Domingo.   Diccionario biográfico americano.
Paris, Tipografía Lahure, 1876.

Destruge, Camilo. Album biográfico ecuatoriano. Guayaquil, Tipografía "El Vigilante" 1904, 4 Vols.

Enciclopedia universal ilustrada europeo-americana. Madrid, Espasa-Calpe S. A., 1907-1930. 70 volumes, ten appendix volumes, annual supplements, 1934-1966.

Erickson, Edwin E., et al. Area Handbook for Ecuador. Washington, U. S. Government Printing Office, 1966, (This is U. S. Government, Department of the Army Publication, DA Pam No. 550-52), 561 pp.

_____. Guía turística del Azuay, 1961. Cuenca: Cámara de Comercio, 1961.

Hilton, Roland. Who's Who in Latin America. Part III. Stanford, California, Stanford University Press, 1951.

Huerta R., Francisco. Atlas escolar del Ecuador. 4th. ed. Guayaquil, Artes Gráficas Senefelder, S. A., 1958.

Lee, Sidney (ed.). Dictionary of National Biography, Index and Epitome, 1850-1901. London, Smith, Elder and Co., 1903.

Metzger, Emil. Geographisch-Statistisches Welt-Lexikon. Stuttgart, Verlag von Felix Krais, 1888.

Moscoso Dávila, Isabel. Abanico de recuerdos. Cuenca, Ecuador, 1970. 182 pp. Biographical sketches of the women of Cuenca, with pen and ink portraits.

Orellana, J. Gonzalo. Patria intellectual. Pequeño album ecuatoriano. Quito, 1915, 195 pp.

Pan American Union. Diccionario de la literatura latino-americana. Ecuador. Washington, D. C., Pan American Union, 1962.

_____. Ecuador, General Descriptive Data. New York, Pan American Union, 1924.

Pérez Marchant, Braulio. Diccionario biográfico del Ecuador. Quito, Escuela de Artes y Oficios, 1928, 515 pp.

_____. Quién es quién en Guayaquil. Guayaquil, Artes Gráficas Senefelder, 1967, 65 pp.
191

_____ . Quién es quién en Quito. Guayaquil, Artes
Gráficas Senefelder, 1966-67, 131 pp.

Scarpetta, M. Leónidas and Saturnino Vergara. Diccionario
biográfico de los campeones de la libertad de Nueva
Granada, Venezuela, Ecuador y Perú. Bogotá, Imprenta de Zalamea, 1879, 728 pp.

Trabucco, Federico E. Síntesis histórica de la República
del Ecuador. Quito, Editorial "Santo Domingo,"
1968, 1117 pp.

Wilgus, A. Curtis. Historical Atlas of Latin America.
Political, Geographic, Economic, Cultural. New York,
Cooper Square Publishers, Inc., 1967. (new and en-
larged edition), XI, 365 pp.